The Five Approaches to Acting Series

PLAYING EPISODES

WRITTEN BY DAVID KAPLAN

Hansen Publishing Group, LLC
East Brunswick, New Jersey
www.hansenpublishing.com

International Standard Book Number: 978-1-60182-182-9

HPG Hansen Publishing Group, LLC
302 Ryders Lane
East Brunswick, New Jersey
732-220-1211
www.hansenpublishing.com

To Edwin W. Schloss,

Prince of friends, open-hearted, open-eyed.

CONTENTS

SCRIPT ANALYSIS COMPARATIVE REFERENCE CHART

	TASK/ACTION ANALYSIS	EPISODIC ANALYSIS	BUILDING IMAGES ANALYSIS	WORLD OF THE PLAY ANALYSIS	NARRATIVE ANALYSIS
BASIC UNIT	Task	Episode	Image	Social context; behavior and form	Event Point of view
ILLUSION OF CHARACTER	Web of relationships	Playing the opposition	String of masks	Distinctions within the context of the world	Intersection of point of view and events
DRAMATIC ACTION	Action meeting an obstacle	Transaction or *gest*	Moment when mask changes	Breach in the rules of the world	Shifting the point of view
KEY QUESTION	What do I need to do?	What do I do? What is my role?	What is this like? What does this make me think of?	What are the values of the world?	What am I describing? What is my point of view?
UNIFYING IMAGE	Oil painting	Poster	Collage	Frame	Film camera angles
RELATIVE THEORY	Freud Psychoanalysis	Alfred Adler Transactional analysis Marxism	Carl Jung Personae	Ruth Benedict Cultural anthropology	Derrida Literary deconstructionism
SUITABLE PLAYWRIGHTS	Chekhov Ibsen Strindberg	Shakespeare Brecht Ionesco	Strindberg Lorca Genet Williams	Molière Wilde O'Neill Beckett	Shakespeare the Greeks Williams Shepard
AUDIENCE	Compassionate	Judgmental	Passionate	Transported	Participatory

PLAYING EPISODES

Reading List
In the Jungle of Cities by Bertolt Brecht
King Richard III by William Shakespeare
Brecht on Theater (section 24) by Bertolt Brecht

Viewing List
The Night of the Hunter directed by Charles Laughton
Raging Bull directed by Martin Scorsese

George Grosz, *Getting the Axe*

CHAPTER 1

EPISODES

The Trouble with Stanislavsky

In 1908, Stanislavsky himself stumbled onto a definition of *episodic acting* after the actress Olga Knipper (who was Chekhov's widow) fled a Moscow Art Theater rehearsal in tears. Knipper was preparing the central role in a revival of Ivan Turgenev's *A Month in the Country*; Stanislavsky was directing her. Turgenev had written the play sixty years before, never expecting his words to be spoken in a theater. More novelist than playwright, Turgenev doubted it was possible to depict the intricacies of behavior outside of fiction and believed his text would be most effective read silently at home. Stanislavsky, however, was eager for the challenge of dramatizing the interior lives of onstage characters and looked forward to the play's inaction, the better to display "a lacework" of psychology (27).

In rehearsal, however, it quickly became apparent that the central role of Natalya Petrovna was as exasperating to her interpreter as she was to the other characters in the play. Natalya Petrovna is a married woman pursued by a devoted admirer. When Natalya Petrovna falls in love with her son's boyish tutor (played by a nineteen-year-old Richard Boleslavsky), she finds herself vying with an inexperienced eighteen-year-old girl (Natalya Petrovna's ward) for the tutor's affections. Natalya Petrovna's behavior is capricious, perverse, contradictory—and very true to life. A hunt for the motives of her caprice was tormenting the actress Olga Knipper as she built the role. Stanislavsky was similarly frustrated directing the play. It was a critical moment for the director and his actress. After two months spent discussing the script without getting out of their chairs, they discovered that their approach had run them into a dead end. Isaiah Berlin writes in the Introduction to his translation of *A Month in the Country*:

> Stanislavsky wrote [Olga Knipper] a famous letter in which he tried to express his understanding of her condition and his profound sympathy with it. She was grateful and comforted. When she finally returned, he explained to her that in his view the play was best acted in sections, that is, without necessary continuity either of mood or tone . . . The part could only be successfully acted by dividing it into segments: in one segment Natalya Petrovna is amusing, charming, enthusiastic, untroubled; in the next segment she is at the beginning of a new mood—jealousy, suspicion, uneasiness, and the like. Other

constant changes of tone, feeling and mood follow, carefully separated from each other . . ." (28)

That's as good a way to begin to define *episodic acting* as any other you'd read: the play is best acted in segments, carefully separated from each other, without continuity.

Why does Natalya Petrovna flirt with the tutor? Bully her ward? Antagonize her lover? Remain with her husband? She doesn't know. Her creator didn't know. Why should a performer pretend to know? In order to release the actress from the crushing responsibility of explaining away the role's inexplicable motivation, Stanislavsky was cornered into organizing the performance into episodes. It worked. Olga Knipper's Natalya Petrovna was deliciously unpredictable.

The rehearsals of *A Month in the Country* provided Stanislavsky with his first opportunity to put his system into practical use while directing and acting in a play. Understandably, he concentrated on the techniques of task, action, and obstacle at the expense of investigating playing separate segments. Soon, though, other theater artists elaborated the techniques of episodic acting, for it had sturdy roots in the most ancient traditions of performing and, paradoxically, satisfied the demands of the twentieth century's avant-garde.

The Basics of an Episode

The skills of episodic acting are crude:

- Figure out what you're supposed to do.
- Do it.
- Make sure the people watching you understand that it happened.

Like telling a story, which it resembles, organizing a performance episodically is a technique so old it's prehistoric, and so basic that it gets reinvented whenever there's a parade or a fourth-grade health pageant. Using definitions given by the British novelist E.M. Forster in his book of lectures, *Aspects of the Novel*:

"The King died and then the Queen died" is a story.
"The King died and then the Queen died of grief" is a plot (29).

What an episodically structured performance does is act out a *story*, or sequence of *events*, rather than attempt to perform a *plot* linked together by cause and effect. In theory, each event in a story can be understood separately from the sequence. *The Queen died*, for example, is an event—no matter if it's due to grief or unlucky coincidence. *The Professor kills his Pupil* is another event, no matter why. Performed onstage—no matter why—an event becomes an *episode*.

Onstage, as in a parade, when episode succeeds episode, unexpected juxtapositions and the mystery of what will happen next create an engaging sequence for an audience.

Often there is a deliberate ambiguity to the connections between episodes in a play—a dramatic ambiguity that the playwright intends. As a literary device, episodic structure organizes anonymous medieval texts, plays by Shakespeare, and texts by twentieth-century playwrights like Bertolt Brecht or Samuel Beckett. Some examples:

- *The Stations of the Cross*
- *The Crimes and Punishment of Richard III*
- *The Business Deals of Mother Courage*
- *What Happens While Waiting for Godot*

While clearly different in tone and intention, these sequences are similar in that they require an actor to *identify and perform a series of events for an audience*.

The Spokesman for Episodes: Bertolt Brecht

Although episodic acting renews itself vigorously whenever it can—even at the sources of motivated acting—it wasn't codified as a system until the middle of the 1930s, when an approach to acting to rival Stanislavsky's was set forth by the brash, opportunistic, and foul-smelling German writer Bertolt Brecht.

Brecht cultivated his odor. He smoked cheap cigars and he seldom bathed. He willfully groomed himself like a truck driver and wore cheap steel-rimmed glasses and a loose leather jacket. Early photographs show him scrawny and bookish, strumming a guitar. Brecht was born in 1898 to a middle-class family. Once he moved from the south of Germany to Berlin, he worked up a coarse, direct way with language, art, and women. Just as Stanislavsky's personal elegance* tells us something about his aesthetic, Brecht's vulgar poses tell us something about his. If Stanislavsky's ambition was to coax the spirit of an actor to soar, Brecht meant to plant an actor's feet firmly into the earth.

These two founders of twentieth-century acting differed in other radical ways. Although he did strum the guitar once or twice for pay, Brecht, unlike Stanislavsky, was never an actor. He began his career in the theater as a writer, part of a generation of German artists who referred to themselves as the primitives of a new era. Their intention was to create art that was coarse, crude, and direct. The title of Brecht's early plays, set in Chicago and Berlin, convey his attitude toward urban life: *In the Jungle of Cities* and *Drums in the Night*. Brecht constructed these texts out of scenes unconnected by cause and effect, and they needed to be staged—like Turgenev's *A Month in the Country*—with an approach to acting very different from Stanislavsky's "psychological lace."

When the Moscow Art Theater played Berlin in the early 1920s, Brecht was in attendance with his musical collaborator Kurt Weill. They were accompanied by, of all people, Isadora Duncan and her boyfriend, the Russian poet Yesenin. During a performance of Chekhov's *Three Sisters*, the four of them dissolved into giggles at the actors'

---

*Stanislavsky's appearance as an elegant gentleman was hard-won. While on tour in Berlin, the financially strapped actor was ashamed to leave his hotel room because his clothes were so shabby.

concentrated effort to maintain the fourth wall. The believable and rounded characters, the illusion of reality—even the audience's compassion—all seemed laughably outdated to Bertolt Brecht (30).

Theater more to Brecht's liking were the plays staged by the daring Berlin director Erwin Piscator* at the Volksbühne ("the People's Stage"), where seats were cheap and the audience smoked. During Volksbühne performances, projectors showed documentary footage and narrators or choruses described the onstage action, even as it was happening. Film, choruses, and actors at the Volksbühne combined forces to tell the story of the play, the modern-day equivalent of a bard reciting an epic around a fire. The actors themselves addressed the public directly so that the experiences of the characters in the play could be understood by the audience *objectively*, not shared in, as Stanislavsky would have wanted. Piscator called these innovations in staging *epic theater.*

In 1927, Brecht was invited to assist Piscator, who was then forming a new theater in Berlin. Brecht worked on texts for Piscator and collaborated in directing the work. But by the next year Brecht and Kurt Weill had written an unexpectedly popular musical play that has since become a standard of the international repertory—*The Threepenny Opera*. Soon after, Brecht began to direct on his own, developing Piscator's experiments in his own way.

In the course of the next thirty years, as a director and writer, Brecht redefined Piscator's epic theater, and under that name developed a system of acting to rival Stanislavsky's. Unfortunately, *epic acting* already means something in English—Elizabeth Taylor as Cleopatra.† We need to use another term. Piscator reclaimed his own identity by renaming his work *objective theater* (*objective* in the sense of *matter-of-fact*, rather than Stanislavsky's translator's fruitful misinterpretation of the Russian word for "tasks" as "objectives"). Other artists used other words to describe similar techniques, among them *constructivist* theater. Whatever the term, all were approaches to organizing a performance into separated events onstage. Let's agree to call them *playing an episode*.

Like Stanislavsky, Brecht wrote essays defining a grammar of terms for performers, gave practical advice to professionals, and suggested exercises for developing the expertise of students. Also like Stanislavsky, he founded a theater—the Berliner Ensemble—where actors were trained in these techniques and directed by Brecht. At home or on tour, the actors of the Berliner Ensemble dazzled audiences with the assured, quiet mastery of their craft.

When he died in 1956 (the cigars?), Brecht left behind five volumes of collected essays and over forty plays. Throughout his life he wrote poetry as well; Brecht the poet is considered to be among the greatest of twentieth-century Germans. Moreover, there is an industry of writing *about* Brecht. His influence as a director and writer is studied, debated, exalted, and reviled. We will concentrate on what can be put into use by actors. But first, in order to appreciate the scope and limits of Brecht's contribution, it's important to understand the circumstances of his time and place.

---

*Pronounced pis-KAH-tor. It's telling that the name of this pivotal yet neglected figure in the American theater is all too often mispronounced.

†D.W. Griffith's *Orphans of the Storm* calls itself an epic, too.

Sources for Brecht

Brecht's work rose on foundations—sometimes credited, sometimes not—laid by others. By force of his personality and persuasive writing, he became the spokesman for episodic acting.

Zola's social novel and roles

To begin with, an actor who organizes a text into episodes defines "character" as a *role* within an onstage action. The question *who are you?* is answered by *what you do*:

- Natalya Petrovna: The Woman Who Flirts with Her Child's Tutor
- Ionesco's Professor: The Teacher Who Kills His Students
- Hedda Gabler: The Unhappy Wife Who Shoots Herself

Fiction, like acting, also proposes models for understanding human relationships. The definition of personality as a role in an episode was anticipated by a particular kind of fiction, the *social novel* of the nineteenth century. Even as it told its story, the social novel also investigated the role of its characters in society. No fiction writer did this more systematically or seriously than the French author Emile Zola. In 1868, around the time when most other novelists were intent on teasing out the nuances of personal motivation, Emile Zola declared that his own writing was meant to establish the "natural laws of society"—that fate and character were functions of environment and heredity. Before he wrote a word, Zola rigorously structured his writing to display how individuals survived or perished due to heredity and social milieu.

Zola lived in poverty for twelve years as he worked on a series of novels depicting the rise and fall of a single family. Not until 1877 did the seventh of the series, a portrait of alcoholics called *L'Assommoir* (the title derived from the French verb *to beat down*—"assommer"), bring him fame and sufficient money.* Despite his lack of popular success, Zola was well thought of by other authors. Turgenev, who lived most of the year in Paris (he wrote *A Month in the Country* there) arranged for a five-year contract for Zola to write short stories for a Russian magazine. The third of the series, "Comment on meurt" ("How One Dies"), was published in August 1876, while Zola was working at his fortune-changing *L'Assommoir*.

There is no plot to "Comment on meurt." There are five separate stories, each a self-contained vignette in which someone dies. Each richly detailed vignette demonstrates how death inevitably takes shape according to class and social position: A Count lies dying with decorum and decency, fastidious and ready to receive visitors. An upper middle-class woman, overhearing her sons planning to divide her estate, goes into her death rattle as she frantically lifts herself up from her sickbed to protest. A shopkeeper's wife dwindles slowly, ruining her health and working all hours to save for the future. A

---

*Three film versions of the story of *L'Assommoir* were made before the First World War; Hollywood borrowed the basic plot for *The Lost Weekend* in 1945.

desperately sick child lies in a fever on a thin mattress; his parents pull tufts of the wool padding out from under him in order to raise enough money for his medicine. A seventy-year-old peasant falls like a tree, ending his life when he has no more strength to work the earth—the same earth into which he is laid as if into a lover's arms. Zola had used this scheme of parallel events among different social classes before in a story called "How One Weds," written for the same Russian magazine.

Zola wanted to lay bare the mechanism of society with the amoral vision of a scientist. No mechanisms of cause and effect are given in the vignettes. The reader is left to conclude for himself how each death is explained by its circumstances. Zola himself found explanations for the mechanism of social evolution in the observations of naturalists. In the forests of the newly industrialized Europe, the fate of an individual white moth trying to hide from birds in a smoke-blackened wood had more to do with the moth's changing environment than with the moth's personal feelings or inclinations. Similarly, according to Zola, the fate of a sick child whose parents couldn't afford medicine, or the life of a woman too overworked to take care of herself, had little to do with their individual actions and a lot more to do with the evolving structure of industrial society.

One of Brecht's earliest published letters (November 10, 1914) "proposes Zola as a model because 'the soul of the people has not yet been explored'" (31). Although Brecht and other twentieth-century advocates of episodic theater disagreed with Zola's explanations of how roles form in society, they did agree that character was not a function of motivations, but could be understood better as a role within a social situation. Three months before Brecht wrote his letter about Zola, the First World War began*—a war that would teach Brecht, and many other people, the insignificance of any individual's actions.

The First World War and after

For many Germans who lived through the First World War, the consequences of personal motivations were shot down in combat and buried for good during the post-war collapse of their society. From 1914 until 1918, in battle after battle, no matter who won, the role of any individual—foot soldier or general—was dwarfed by the destructive power of modern weapons. The weapons' increased capacity to kill so outpaced the capabilities of leaders to command or troops to resist that the number and rapidity of casualties in the First World War still shock today—even with our knowledge of Hiroshima and the Holocaust. Let one battle serve as an example for them all.

It was the summer of the second year of combat, July 1, 1916. As an early light rain gave way to brilliant sunshine along the sluggish Somme River in northern France, twenty thousand men died in battle—ten thousand of them within the first hour of combat, and most of those *in the first few minutes* of the fighting (32). When a soldier faced machine guns firing six hundred bullets a minute, personal traits like bravery, heroism, commitment, and passion, while admirable in some abstract sense, had no real signifi-

---

*The first week of August 1914.

cance. Cowardice, fear, and selfishness had no real significance either, except perhaps as low-level survival skills.

A poem called "Lament" by the British writer F.S. Flint (33) captures a generation's sense of being coerced to play a role in this episode of history. Any personal feelings the actors playing this role might have had really didn't matter:

> The young men of the world
> Are condemned to death.
> They have been called up to die
> For the crime of their fathers . . .
> They have been cast for a cruel purpose
> Into the mashing-press and furnace.
>
> The young men of the world
> No longer possess the road:
> The road possesses them.
> They no longer inherit the earth:
> The earth inherits them.
> They are no longer the masters of fire:
> Fire is their master . . . .

Bombs flew overhead from far-off cannons, poison gas seeped quietly and invisibly into lungs. That the source of death was unseen added to one's sense of powerlessness. A son, a farm, a life's work—all could be destroyed, impersonally, in seconds. Individual action seemed as consequential as the efforts of a white moth trying to hide on a smoke-blackened tree.

Piscator always claimed that his experiences in the war forever sparked his work in the theater. He was drafted as a soldier when he was seventeen. At the first order to fire, he froze in fear and blurted out, as if it were an excuse, that he was an actor. He spent the rest of his life—he says—trying to live down his shame by making his trade socially responsible. Brecht, who was younger, was drafted into the German army in 1918 and ended up as an orderly in a military hospital ward for venereal diseases. A famous poem of his describes (in bouncy verse) how the doctors, in order to put more bodies on the frontlines, would certify even the dead as fit for battle.

When the war ended in November of 1918, Germany lost territory, self-respect, and military strength. Under pressure from the winning side to pay war damages, the German economy collapsed. Brecht first came to Berlin in 1923, but he nearly starved to death and left in three weeks. He was lucky he had a home in the south to escape to. In the city, crowds begged on the streets and scavenged the carcasses of dead horses (34). They were further demoralized by their inability to save their children from a similar fate. Like the soldiers in the First World War—or characters in a social novel by Zola—they were compelled to play roles assigned to them by society.

Artists' response to the social crisis

As soon as the war ended, German painters, architects, composers, industrial designers, playwrights, and stage directors (including Brecht and Piscator) banded together and proclaimed they would dedicate their work to the necessity—and opportunity—of building a new and better world. In the context of the social crisis, making art was recognized as a trade among other trades, not unlike manufacturing. An artist assembled raw materials, produced a finished product, and—just like any other worker—was poorly compensated for his hard work and skill. A quote from Bernard Meyers's *The German Expressionists: A Generation in Revolt* (35) sums it up:

> We painters and poets are bound to the poor in a sacred solidarity. Have not many among us learned to know misery and shame of hunger?

In Weimar, in the south of Germany, a new school of industrial design rose to meet the challenge of rebuilding after the war. It was called the Bauhaus and it took as its spiritual mission the reshaping of this new world. The Bauhaus took full advantage of the technical abilities of mass production to redesign common articles, including soup spoons, and looked to machines for aesthetic inspiration. The designer/craftsman/artist's task was to retool machines to produce new products and, ultimately, new people. Brecht would repeat this idea in his poetry and plays for the rest of his life.

Mass production of art, which had always lessened the value of an art object in the past, now enhanced value because it made it possible for art to reach a mass audience. In order to reach a wide group of people, the forms of art were made simpler to comprehend. No longer was there a need for cultural references that required an expensive education in order to be understood. No longer were shabby clothes and hollow eyes just picturesque details in novels or paintings. Now these images provoked a response among readers and viewers who themselves were poor and hungry.

Sculptors were no longer content to carve marble and cast bronze; they began to assemble the overlooked detritus of everyday life into their work. The sculptor Kurt Schwitters assembled cardboard box tops, newspapers, the soles of shoes, and tin cans—even the valueless German currency (which was probably the cheapest paper one could get).

In Russia, Moscow was undergoing a similar reorganization politically and artistically after the Russian Revolution, which ended at roughly the same time as the First World War. Cultural exchange between Berlin and Moscow was direct and strong at this time, and mass production and the virtues of industry were the trade secrets Moscow had to offer. The Russian sculptor El (for Eliezor) Lessitsky brought the aesthetic of gear shafts and pistons to Berlin. The Hungarian artist László Moholy-Nagy (pronounced NADJ) designed the curriculum at the Bauhaus, educating the next generation of German artists in the Russian approach. Russian experiments in theatrical form, begun by a renegade disciple of Stanislavsky's named Vsevolod Meyerhold, set off a response in the German theater world as well. At first the experiments were in stagecraft and scenery: Moholy-Nagy designed sets for Piscator with turntables, treadmills, slide projections, and machine parts. There were more innovations to come.

The example of Georg Grosz

Close ties between visual and theater artists helped to transform avant-garde German theater. Among the most influential visual artists was the painter Georg Grosz. Although he worked in watercolor and oil, Grosz was best known for his lithographs and black-ink drawings. He also designed scenery for Piscator, and almost went to jail over one of his backdrops. Grosz knew Brecht from the start; he'd illustrated Brecht's poem of the doctor sending a rotting corpse to the war front.

That particular sketch was one of a series that Grosz drew between 1918 and 1926, and published in Berlin in 1930, under the title *The Marked Men (Die Gezeichneten)*. The collection begins with a quote from the Bible (Genesis 1:28): *And God said to them be fruitful and multiply and subdue the earth.* With a ruthless, unblinking eye and superb technique, Grosz illustrated the multiple ways Berliners had subdued the earth—and each other. In the drawings, women of all ages sell themselves, unkempt unemployed men loiter on street corners, and a rich man hauls bread out of the reach of poor children.

Grosz's work usually depicts a relationship between people—just like good acting. Background scenery is rudimentary: a wall, a potted plant, a window (in which, often enough, a murder is being committed). Yet the essential details of class that define people's social roles are etched with precision: the expensive silk underwear of the whores, the crisp striped cravat tied around Hitler's neck, the stubble on the faces of the poor.

No single plot connects the pictures. Like the scenes of an episodic play, each of the sixty plates is a little scene complete in itself: a poor family contemplates the goods it cannot buy, an ax murderer washes his bloody hands at the kitchen sink, a bloated old man eyes a bare-breasted young girl. Often the scenes have a central *gesture*. In one sketch, for example, a well-fed dandy lifts his well-shod foot to avoid the artificial leg of a war veteran who is begging in the street. This is captioned, by the way: *Don't Trip!*

The devices of Grosz's lithographs—social roles, episodic tableaux, essential gestures, captions, cartoonish distortions mixed with precise realistic details—paralleled Piscator's and Brecht's techniques in creating the devices of modern episodic acting. Many of Grosz's drawings are captioned because they first appeared in newspapers and needed to be quickly and easily understood by a wide mass of readers (who were no less connoisseurs of everyday life than wealthy collectors of oil paintings). The captions summed up the action of each little scene in the same way that banners or actors announced the title of an episode directly to the audience in episodic theater productions.

Even the degree of finish of Grosz's drawings was influential. Grosz spattered, scratched, dropped, and dragged the ink across the nubby surface of the paper. His lines were spare and spiky. His images had a job to communicate directly, simply, and immediately; they didn't need the careful modeling and creamy finish of oil painting. The deliberate distortions and use of simplified and cartoonish effects were sufficient to animate the scene and clarify the episode on the paper. Episodic acting was similarly bold. Brecht and Piscator had their actors mix distortions with the precise details of observed behavior to achieve a style of acting more real than realism.

Rival episodic theater: politics

During this period in Germany, distraction was as necessary as bread. Episodic entertainments such as circuses, pageants, and musical reviews were very popular—and easier to sit through than classical theater or a composed symphony. But even some twentieth-century operas were episodic in structure: both Richard Strauss's *Elektra* (1909) and Alban Berg's *Wozzeck* (1925)* had librettos comprised of scenes that depicted unrelated incidents rather than aspects of one continuous plot.

Other, more sinister episodes were being staged in Brecht and Piscator's Berlin as well—and not on the stage. As drama became more political, politics became more dramatic. In stadiums and open squares, Nazi rallies and parades were essentially staged performances that used techniques similar to those used by Piscator's People's Stage. They even copied the look of his posters. Rallies featured speeches clarified by banners and slogans. Arms outstretched in salute were effective essential gestures. Historical and current events were presented as simply as possible, with roles assigned to individuals and ethnic groups.

In 1932, Nazi thugs staged a real-life episode by burning Berlin's parliament building—then acting out the role of Innocent Victim. In the next episode, the Nazis, playing the role of Protector, seized control of the central government and cast their opponents in the role of Criminals. Piscator, Brecht, Grosz, and Weill fled the country—as did other intellectuals and artists, including Albert Einstein, Sigmund Freud, and Marlene Dietrich.

Inspiration: Mei Lanfang

Brecht and Piscator—in exile from Germany—separately made their wandering ways to Russia. Piscator had visited the Soviet Union first in 1931, directing a film and helping to organize a German-speaking theater in a part of Central Asia then called the Volga German Republic, now Kazakhstan; although he was too busy at the time to go there. In the spring of 1935, Brecht and Piscator were both in Moscow at the time the great Chinese actor Mei Lanfang was performing there on tour.

Mei Lanfang played only women's roles. He performed only in Mandarin Chinese. Usually, his make-up was an elaborate pink and white mask that took two hours to apply. His touring repertory was comprised almost exclusively of scenes from the traditional Peking opera.† In Peking opera roles, Mei Lanfang's costumes were intricately stylized, so much so that the costume could be used to set the scene. Aside from the costume, Mei Lanfang appeared onstage without scenery, except for two chairs and a table. In order to be understood by audiences who didn't share the language of his texts, his performance was organized to present one complete event that could be understood from the beginning of the scene to the end: *The Concubine Forsakes the Losing General,*

---

*Based on *Woyzeck*, a series of fragmentary scenes written by Georg Büchner in 1837, unpublished until 1879.

†He also played shop girls—but never abroad.

for example. The Chinese film *Farewell My Concubine* (1993, directed by Chen Kaige) shows just such a scene, by the way, performed by students of students of Mei Lanfang.

Mei Lanfang's technical skill was such that he became his own cooperative ensemble. He could play two roles at once: his legs and feet could play the horse he was riding, while the upper part of his body could perform the rider's emotions and expressions. Like Grosz's drawings, details of precise realism were simultaneously juxtaposed with stylization. Like the Bauhaus aesthetic, Mei Lanfang's craft was openly on display; he could be seen watching his own gestures. The audience was invited to notice the artificiality of the acting and appreciate the craft necessary to act the onstage event.

At his first Moscow appearance Mei Lanfang had the assurance to perform out of make-up, in a dinner jacket. Brecht went to watch—and he didn't giggle. He was entranced. So were Meyerhold and, by the way, Stanislavsky. Meyerhold was captivated by the vocabulary of gestures and the elegant, streamlined stagecraft. What appealed to Stanislavsky was that the performer's inner commitment, like Duse's, was manifest in beauty and grace. Piscator, on the other hand, dismissed it as oriental exotica. As for Brecht, just as Stanislavsky was inspired by Salvini and Duse to form his ideas on motivated acting, so too was Brecht now inspired by Mei Lanfang to form concrete ideas about epic acting (distinct from epic *staging*). When he saw the Chinese actor perform, Brecht recognized the possibility of a systematic acting style that could fulfil his episodic plays—and revolutionize acting in the West.

Terms to Work with: Episodes and Captions

Brecht's definitions are buried amid charts and essays. Often they have to be deduced. Late in life, after rereading his own writing, Brecht realized he'd left out the most obvious principles. As we did with Stanislavsky's terms, let's agree on some basic terms for *episodic acting* in order to put them into practical use. In 1936, after his first trip to New York, Brecht wrote to Piscator: ". . . it's quite wrong that we should be making no propaganda for our view of theater and film. We ought to write articles, possibly an illustrated booklet, all this mass of material must at last be got into shape and made usable. I read Stanislavsky's *My Life in Art* with unease mixed with envy. The man got his system straight, with the result that in Paris and New York everyone's becoming a Stanislavsky disciple. Is that unavoidable?" (36).

Episode

An **episode** is an event performed onstage that is understood by its audience complete and by itself, separate from the whole of the play. Some examples:

- Natalya Petrovna flirts with the tutor.
- The Professor stumps the Pupil.
- The Professor stomps the Pupil.
- The Chinese Princess leaves her King.

The relationships between actors in an episode always imply the relationship between the actors and the audience. The essence of an episode is that something changes in the course of its playing, and the audience notices that it has changed.

As in good industrial design, all aspects of the performance—scenery, costumes, lighting, even the acting—are parts of a machine designed to perform the episode. It is not necessary to convince the audience that they are watching anything other than performers on stage. Any means of getting the episode across to the public is legitimate.

Caption

For purposes of analysis for actors, episodes are captioned. Like newspaper headlines, or the titles of Grosz's lithographs, an actor's **caption** for an episode should paraphrase or sum up the onstage event. A good caption is in the form of a complete sentence: it includes a subject, a verb, and object. A caption should answer the questions:

- What happens?
- Who makes it happen?
- To whom does it happen?

For example: HEDDA REVOLTS is insufficient as a caption because it is vague. HER SPIRIT IS FREED is not much better. What that will produce onstage is a tableau vivant. Better is: HEDDA REVOLTS AGAINST HER HUSBAND'S WORLD. Or: HEDDA DECLINES TO JOIN HER HUSBAND'S WORLD. HEDDA SHOOTS HERSELF is good, too, especially if you can avoid the temptation to explain why. Headlines out of sensationalist newspapers are a good model for the style of a caption (but not necessarily the style of your performance): MANIAC PROF OFFS STAR PUPIL. WIFE'S EX VISITS HONEYMOON COUPLE.

A caption can also answer *when* and *where*, but it does not include *how* and *why*. The *how* will be demonstrated onstage. *Why* is immaterial, or will be deduced by the audience. At first, the episodes in a rehearsal will usually be identified as brief units. After repetition in rehearsal—and performance—these smaller episodes will coalesce into larger ones.

Applying Episodic Techniques: Rehearsing a Scene from *In the Jungle of Cities*

Let's continue illustrating episodic techniques as if we were rehearsing the first scene of Bertolt Brecht's *In the Jungle of Cities* (1922) (37). This is from the playwright's prologue:

> *You are in Chicago in 1912. You will witness an inexplicable wrestling match between two men and observe the downfall of a family that has moved from the prairies to the jungle of the big city. Don't worry your head about the motives for the fight, keep your minds on the stakes. Judge impartially the technique of the contenders, and be prepared to concentrate on the finish.*

This scene begins with the central character, Garga, alone onstage, quietly working in the library wrapping books.

> SKINNY If we read the sign right, this is a lending library. We'd like to borrow a book.
>
> GARGA What kind of a book?
>
> SKINNY A fat one.
>
> GARGA For yourself?
>
> SKINNY (*who looks at* SHLINK *before each answer*) No, not for me, for this gentleman.
>
> GARGA Your name?
>
> SKINNY Shlink, lumber dealer, 6 Mulberry Street.
>
> GARGA (*taking down name*) Five cents a week per book. Take your pick.
>
> SKINNY No, you choose one.
>
> GARGA This is a detective story, it's not good. Here's something better—a travel book.
>
> SKINNY Just like that you say the book is no good?
>
> SHLINK (*stepping up to him*) Is that your personal opinion? I'll buy your opinion. Is ten dollars enough?
>
> GARGA Take it as a gift.

Why does Shlink, a bully of a lumber dealer, want to buy the clerk's opinion? The reason is not important, the playwright says, just pay attention to what happens. Garga refuses to sell.

Identifying roles

Why does Skinny look at Shlink before each answer? In an episodic structure an actor does not so much play a character as take a **role** in the episode (Bully or Bookworm). The question is not so much *Who am I?* as it is *What do I do?* or *How does it fit in with what other people do?* In order for the episode to work, its roles must interconnect. There is a theater game where actors pretend to be parts of a machine—making noises and swinging their arms, or twisting their bodies like a clockwork made of human beings. This exercise is a metaphor for what must happen onstage: that all the actors play roles that fit together like the parts of a machine in order to produce the effect of the episode.

In *In the Jungle of Cities*, Shlink is the Man Who Wants to Buy an Opinion. Garga is the Man Who Refuses Him. Skinny is the Man Who Speaks for Shlink. If you play Skinny, it is a noble waste of time to figure out *why* you speak for Shlink. Looking at Shlink before he speaks makes Skinny's role clear to the audience. Skinny is the role of the Man Who Speaks for Shlink.

> SHLINK You mean you've changed your opinion and now it's a good book?
>
> GARGA No.

PLAYING EPISODES

SKINNY Ten dollars will buy you some fresh clothes.

GARGA My job here is wrapping books, that's all.

SKINNY It drives the customers away.

GARGA What do you want of me? I don't know you. I've never seen you before.

As rehearsals progress, roles will be defined fully from the beginning to end of the play:

- I'm the Pupil Who Gets Killed.
- I'm the Maniacal Teacher Who Kills His Pupil to Teach Her a Lesson.
- I'm the Woman Trapped in a Bourgeois Marriage.
- I'm the Husband Who Wishes His Wife Were More Like Other Men's Wives.

At first in rehearsal, the roles will be simpler:

- I'm the Bully.
- I'm the Bully's Henchman.
- I'm the Innocent Man Wrapping Books.

Similarly, you will begin with a rough draft of a caption. For example:

BULLY TRIES TO BRIBE THE BOOKWORM

GARGA I never heard of this book and it doesn't mean a thing to me.

SHLINK I'm offering you forty dollars for your opinions of it.

GARGA I'll sell you the opinions of Mr. J.V. Jensen and Mr. Arthur Rimbaud but I won't sell you my own opinion.*

SHLINK Your opinion is just as worthless as theirs, but right now I want to buy it.

GARGA I indulge in opinions.

SHLINK Are your family millionaires?

GARGA My family lives on rotten fish.

SHLINK (obviously pleased) A fighter! I'd have expected you to come across with the words that would give me pleasure and get your family something better than fish.

By the end of this scene, the thoughtful Garga has been provoked into a reckless fight. That's the outcome of the entire scene, but it will take us time to get there.

---

*The references are to books Brecht was reading at the time he wrote the play: the French writer Arthur Rimbaud's *A Season in Hell* (part template for Brecht's idea of Chicago) and the Danish novelist J. V. Jensen's *The Wheel*, a homosexual murder story set in Chicago. One of Brecht's early notes indicates that Garga should resemble Rimbaud in appearance and Garga's love/hate relationship with Shlink should parallel Rimbaud's stormy relationship with the poet Verlaine.

SKINNY Forty bucks! That's a lot of fresh shirts for you and your family.

GARGA I'm not a prostitute.

SHLINK (*with humor*) I hardly think my fifty dollars interferes with your inner life.

GARGA Raising your offer is one more insult and you know it.

SHLINK (*naïvely*) A man's got to know which is better, a pound of fish or an opinion. Or two pounds of fish or the opinion.

SKINNY Dear sir, your stubbornness will get you into trouble.

GARGA I'm going to have you thrown out.

SKINNY Having opinions shows you don't know anything about life.

Report to the audience

In order to make the episode clearer, this last line of Skinny's could be said directly to the audience. In fact, without the barrier of a fourth wall, much of the scene could be directed to the audience in order to clarify the episode. Skinny can show the audience the money offered to Garga, bill by bill, before he sticks the cash under Garga's nose. Many of Garga's lines can be delivered directly to the audience:

- *My job here is wrapping books, that's all.*
- *I never heard of this book and it doesn't mean a thing to me.*
- *I indulge in opinions.*
- *My family lives on rotten fish.*
- *I'm not a prostitute.*

As can both of the following:

SHLINK A man's got to know which is better, a pound of fish or an opinion.

SKINNY Having opinions shows you don't know anything about life.

This direct contact with the audience breaks one of Stanislavsky's rules that contribute to the illusion of the stage: that the actors behave with each other and ignore the audience. In one of his essays, Piscator dismisses Stanislavsky's example of actors ignoring the audience in a hunt for a dropped nail or a lost shoe, and adds that he himself is always embarrassed when actors looking out to the audience pretend not to notice the hundreds of staring eyes.

Demonstration

Brecht once gave his definition of good epic acting by saying it would be like watching the actor who plays Hamlet teaching his understudy what to do, late at night in the theater, while both are a little drunk. Imagine what that "Hamlet" says: "Okay, in this scene you get down on your knees, and you pick up the skull real slow. You say the first word,

'Alas,' then you make the audience wait while you think of something really sad, then you turn the skull toward them and continue the line (*mournful sigh, followed by a hiccup*) 'Poor Yorick.'"

The actor playing Hamlet is giving his understudy a **demonstration**.

Demonstration is different from enactment and its rules of good taste are different, too. Asides, indicating, direct address, playing to the house are—when playing an episode—no longer cheap theatrics and in bad taste. Properly done, they call attention not to the actor, but to the events of the play. Cartoons, exaggerations, and dismantling the illusion that the actor is a different person are anathema to Stanislavsky's aesthetic. In episodic theater, however, whatever makes the episode clear is appropriate. Just as the drunken actor demonstrates Hamlet's believable confusion, episodic theater has a place for realistic behavior and motivation. It also drops those things when it is effective to do so.

Demonstration is not meant to move the audience in the same way as enactment. Brecht and Piscator said the actor should prod the audience to judge the action, not seduce them into sharing the character's emotions. Empathy would confuse the audience about what was going on.

This desire not to be caught up in the emotion of a crowd was not a personal quirk of Brecht's or Piscator's; keeping one's head in the middle of pandemonium was a strategy for survival. The best-attended theatrical events in Berlin were Nazi rallies, parades, and public meetings that fully exploited the techniques of swaying the emotions of a crowd. If the theater trained people to be receptive to emotions without thinking, if the theater got people in the habit of being moved by captivating speakers, then tyrants like Hitler would be in power forever. Theatergoing would be one of those perverse ceremonies of a culture—like witch-burning and public hangings—that enjoys a long and rich performance history throughout the world.

Brecht and Piscator wanted a theater where what happened onstage and offstage would be questioned rather than wept at or laughed over. That doesn't mean the theater's emotions are taken away; it means emotions are not an end in themselves. "Are you enjoying this?" Garga asks the audience. The audience is meant to ask itself the same question.

In fact, in the best of all possible worlds, you play an episode to the little old matinee ladies in the balcony who have joined your grandmother for a theater weekend in the city. (They're staying at a hotel in midtown and they've just had Salad Niçoise for lunch.) You want those happy ladies sitting in the balcony to shout out in piercing voices: "Oh, look, he's minding his own business when that strange man comes in and picks a fight." It's a confirmation of good episodic acting when the ladies in the balcony comment on what's happening onstage and say the episode's caption aloud. "Will that librarian take the money?" "Turn him down!" "That Skinny is a pest." "Oh! *I* get it! Shlink wants to buy his soul."*

As the scene progresses, another caption may suggest itself:

---

*Brecht himself wrote dialogue critiquing his play *Man = Man*. Fake matinee ladies saying these lines in the audience can turn a performance of *Man = Man* into an impromptu debate over the play's merits.

PEACEFUL MAN DRAWN INTO VIOLENT STRUGGLE TO SURVIVE

GARGA I'm going to have you thrown out.

SKINNY Having opinions shows you don't know anything about life.

SHLINK Miss Larry says you wanted to go to Tahiti!

GARGA How do you know Jane Larry?

SHLINK She's starving. She's not getting paid for the shirts she sews. You haven't been to see her in three weeks.

GARGA *drops a pile of books.*

Why does Garga drop the books? Is he nervous? Angry? Just drop the books. The sound they make hitting the floor will alert the balcony to pay attention. Let *them* argue why you dropped the books.

SKINNY Watch your steps! You're only an employee.

GARGA You're molesting me. But there's nothing I can do about it.

SHLINK You're poor.

GARGA I live on fish and rice. You know that as well as I do.

SHLINK Sell!

SKINNY Are you an oil king?

SHLINK The people in your neighborhood feel sorry for you.

GARGA I can't shoot down the whole neighborhood.

SHLINK Your family that came from the prairies . . .

GARGA Sleep three in a bed by a broken drain pipe. I smoke at night, it's the only way I can get to sleep. The windows are closed because Chicago is cold. Are you enjoying this?

That last line can be spoken directly to the audience, who, freed from the responsibility of suspending disbelief at what they are watching, are allowed to think about what they enjoy.

Transactions

Zola's model for the mechanism of roles in society was natural science; Brecht's model for roles derived from economic science. Brecht shared a worldview that all forms of human behavior—onstage and off—were functions of power and commerce, and essentially political. "Political" aspects of power and commerce are inherent in all human relationships. The founders of twentieth-century episodic acting would all have agreed that an actor's performance should bring such political aspects into focus for an audience. Working with this approach, an episode includes an additional set of questions related to **transactions**:

- What is being bought or sold?
- Who is the buyer?
- Who is the seller?
- What is the price?
- Is the deal concluded?

Sell! says Shlink. Just what is Shlink buying when he offers forty dollars for Garga's "opinion"? Is the price fair? The answers to these questions organize the first scene of *In the Jungle of Cities* much better than any investigation of the character's inscrutable motives.

The *gest*

In order to fully reveal the episode, the moment that the deal is concluded or fails has to be made clear onstage. Let's agree to call this playing the **gest,** from the same root word as for *gesture.* Think of it as the *gist* of the scene. Better yet, think of the moment of the *gest* as the photograph in the tabloid that would accompany the episode's headline. Yet the *gest* is not frozen in time, like a tableau; a *gest* implies the movement of an offer, an exchange, or a rejection.

A *gest* always involves a human gesture, an interaction between at least two people—or in some cases, two aspects of one person's character. It's different from the *psychological gesture* of Michael Chekhov, mentioned in Chapter 3, which is personal, symbolic, and without political content. For Brecht and Piscator, all *gests* had social significance, which for them implied politics, and, according to their notion of politics, *commerce.* The smallest social unit, Brecht claimed, was *two.*

caption	*gest*
SHLINK OFFERS GARGA MONEY FOR HIS OPINION	Skinny sticks the money under Garga's nose. Garga turns his head away.
HEDDA BURNS LOVE OUT OF HER HEART	She flings the manuscript into the fireplace.
THE PROFESSOR STUMPS THE PUPIL	His finger in her face, her eyes crossed.
THE PROFESSOR STOMPS THE PUPIL	His body coming within inches of her face, but never touching her.

*The contradictory and convoluted definitions of *gest* or *gestus* are, in part, what prevent Brecht's ideas from being applied by working actors. It does not further the cause of propaganda to repeat, as Peter Thomson does in "Brecht and Actor Training" from *Twentieth Century Acting Training* (38), "Gestus is 'the aesthetic gestural presentation of the economic and socio-ideological construction of human identity and interaction,' something which 'finds ultimate expression in the corporeal and intellectual work of the performer.' " Try saying that in a rehearsal.

At the beginning of *In the Jungle of Cities*, Garga is quietly wrapping books as Shlink and Skinny lurk in the door of the lending library. This could be the first tableau for *In the Jungle of Cities*. At the end of the first scene the library is a shambles. Shlink and Skinny stand amidst the wreckage, Garga is gone. In case the ladies in the balcony missed the point of the scene, Skinny will tell them: *We finally drove him out of his skin*. The *gest* might be the moment Garga threw his coat and shoes to the ground and ran out barefoot.

Would-be directors, take note: the episode can be given its essential structure by staging in rehearsal a tableau of the scene's beginning, a tableau of the scene's end, and the *gest* in between. Draw little sketches with stick figures, if you like. Just as you can rehearse a scene in order to uncover and elaborate its motivations, you can rehearse a scene with the intention of discovering the *gest*, or, once it's discovered, polishing the *gest*.

Very good examples of *gests* are in Grosz's cartoons, of course.

A *gest* can include a prop. In fact, the use of props in episodic technique is called, by Brecht, the **object lesson**. The object, onstage, represents an essential part of the episode, and is understood by the audience in this way. Hedda *burning Løvborg's manuscript* or the civilized Garga *tearing off his shoes* are good examples. The resemblance of the *gest* to the poses of melodrama are what make *gests* so potent in an object lesson. *Gests* and object lessons are sometimes given by the playwright, but very often you will rehearse the scene hoping to discover an effective *gest* with which to play the scene.

With the use of effective episodes and *gests*, the performance should be understandable apart from the language in which the play is being performed. This is not to rob the words of their theatrical power. Just the opposite, it gives the words the dramatic structure necessary to achieve theatrical power. The lack of such a structure is the problem with an approach based exclusively on tasks. If all you are doing is pursuing your task, you can become selfish, not as a character, but as a ham whose self-centeredness diverts the scene from its point, or gist, or—as you now know to call it—episode.

Let's Review Terms

episode	an event played out onstage that is understood by the audience independently of the play
role	your job in performing the episode
transaction	the underlying structure of behavior; trade: something is bought or sold
caption	the summary of the event in the episode
demonstration	making the episode clear to the audience
gest	the moment between people when the trade is made or denied
the object lesson	use of a physical object to demonstrate the gest

The Chart

The chart compares five different ways of organizing and analyzing a text. Let's begin to fill in the categories for *Episodic Analysis*: basic unit, key question, and dramatic action.

- **Basic unit.** The basic unit for the actor is the *episode*, an event that happens onstage, understood by the audience.
- **Key question.** The key question for an actor to answer in an episode is *What do I do?*
- **Dramatic action.** The dramatic action is defined as a *transaction* between characters, clarified by a *gest* at the moment when the transaction is successfully completed or falls apart.

CHAPTER 2

COMBINING EPISODES

Playing an Opposition

When a character performs a role in an episode reluctantly—his reactions at odds with his actions even as he performs them—that is called *playing an opposition*. Some examples:

- Hedda Gabler weeps as she destroys Løvborg's manuscript.
- Shlink apologizes sincerely for the pain he causes Garga.
- Skinny politely dumps the library books on the floor.

When a role played in one episode contradicts another of the same character's roles in other episodes, that too, is playing an opposition. Some examples:

- Hamlet plots to avenge his father; Hamlet hesitates when he might kill.
- Hamlet is in love with Ophelia; Hamlet pushes Ophelia off his lap.
- Natalya Petrovna defends her marriage; Natalya Petrovna competes with her ward for the love of her ward's tutor.

As Olga Knipper and Stanislavsky discovered in their rehearsals for *A Month in the Country*, playing **oppositions** frees actors from thinking that inconsistent behavior is a puzzle to be solved by the revelation of consistent need. Playing oppositions makes incongruity fun, not a problem; the tension of contradiction makes such theater theatrical.

The contradictions among a series of roles in an episodic performance create depth in the illusion of a character.

- Ionesco's Professor would like to please his Pupil. The Professor kills the Pupil.
- Hedda Gabler loves Løvborg, burns his manuscript, lies to him, and kills herself.
- Natalya Petrovna, a kind mother, fickle wife, and cruel mistress, flirts with a boy.

When actors demonstrate the kindness of a cruel action, or the harshness of doing good, they are playing oppositions. Performers have done it for centuries, acting on an artist's instinct to give shading to what otherwise would be flat. For a performance that is organized episodically, opposition does more than create interest; it provokes the audience to respond to the text and participate in the performance.

With oppositions left raw and unblended, the reconciliation of opposites (or lack of reconciliation) is left to be done by the audience—not the characters or the actors or the playwright or the director. The dramatic tension between the opposing forces invites such a synthesis. For those who like to use the stage as a tool for expanding social consciousness, the synthesis of oppositions is completed by the actions of the audience after it leaves the theater.

Even without social commitment, the technique of playing an opposition works with episodic structure to build depth for characters and suspense during performances. The use of opposition is meant to provoke the audience to stand apart from any one side of the opposition—including the feelings of any one character—in order to respond to the dynamic of the opposed forces.

Oppositions may sound like Stanislavsky's obstacles, but they aren't. An obstacle interrupts the pursuit of a task, altering actions. Oppositions coincide with each other. They do not blend or interrupt each other; they run parallel. An actor's job is to play each aspect of an opposition so that it holds its own in creating dynamic tension. You hope the combinations that create oppositions add up to something unexpectedly different from the sum of the parts, the way fire and water, carefully brought together, make steam.

Alienation

Alienation is the term Brecht used to describe the process by which actors playing episodes establish *gests*, transactions, and oppositions. What Brecht meant by alienation is to take something familiar, especially familiar human behavior, and *alienate* it from its surroundings so that it seems strange, or alien.* This, in part, was the reason for the captions and labels of epic productions: to get the audience to alienate events and concentrate on the circumstances that produced them. The crash of the books on the floor during the scene from *In the Jungle of Cities* would do the same thing.

For Brecht, alienation does NOT mean shining bright lights in the audience's eyes. It does NOT mean playing ear-splitting music. In fact, it doesn't have anything, anything, *anything* to do with alienating *the audience*. Anyone who tells you that is wrong. Not slightly incorrect. Wrong. Because of the confusion from the word *alienate*, some translators use another term, *estrangement*. But in the English-speaking theater, *estrangement*—like the phrase *epic acting*—already means something related to Elizabeth Taylor: what happened between the actress and most of her husbands. Some translators substitute the coded terms *A-affect* or *E-affect* for *A*-lienation or *E*-strangement. This is

---

*The German word is a translation of the term "alienation," coined by the Russian literary critic Viktor Shklovsky, who used the term to define Tolstoy's technique of describing the familiar as a collection of oddities. Brecht probably learned the word, an uncommon one in German, from his translator during Brecht's second trip to Moscow.

like calling Mrs. Siddons's legs her *limbs*. Let's agree here to call the process alienation—and promise not to shine lights in the audience's eyes.*

When an actor takes what is commonplace, everyday behavior and makes it worthy of aesthetic consideration, that fits the definition of alienation—*making the familiar strange*. Onstage, we alienate casual gestures like shaking hands, signing a deed, tipping the head, or bowing, so that they become significant to the audience. This way they may contribute to the episode. Some alienated gestures even move up the ladder to *gest*.

American Pop Art includes memorably witty examples of alienation. By framing an enlarged Campbell's soup can label or copying the graphics of a Brillo box, Andy Warhol called attention to the aesthetic of commercialized America. Roy Lichtenstein's use of cartoon style and cartoon imagery, including Donald Duck, is another illustration of alienation of the familiar. Then there is Claes Oldenburg, whose sculpture of a lipstick was so huge that its resemblance to a missile was unmistakable enough to draw protests during the Vietnam War. Oldenburg made giant toilet seats, too, and colossal hamburgers and teabags; the more mundane, the more worth looking at again.

The alienation of commonplace objects in Pop Art is a model for behavior alienated onstage: made strange, significant, and worthy of scrutiny. In this way, shoving a pile of books on the floor politely can be understood—by the audience—as an opposition. The Pupil's reflex parroting of nonsense phrases can be understood—by the audience—as a transaction. The nod of Shlink's chin toward the servile Skinny can be understood—by the audience—as a *gest*.

Even a structure of actions and obstacles can be alienated—in order to include realistic behavior within an episode. Because it is alienated, like the words of a quotation inside a larger paragraph—"Say what?"†—the action in pursuit of a task may come to an abrupt end once the episode is over. Brecht urged actors to understand and exploit this sophisticated combination of tasks within episodes.

The combination of objectives within episodes is also what Stanislavsky used for the 1909 rehearsals of *A Month in the Country*. Twenty-five years later, Stanislavsky again played in rehearsal with the technique of organizing a play into segments of action, this time perhaps adapting his system to include the innovations of Meyerhold. Stanislavsky wrote to his son in 1935: "We break the whole play, episode by episode, into physical actions . . ." (39)

The resemblance of Stanislavsky's 1934–1938 rehearsal techniques to episodic acting is striking in other ways, but the essential difference—the unconnected playing of events—was *not* part of Stanislavsky's technique. Stanislavsky's letter to his son goes on to stress that the episodes are rehearsed through improvisations until they look believable and establish a line. That line included cause and effect, rising and falling action, and other devices of *plot*, not story. Oppositions are understood to be *counter-actions* to be overcome, not played simultaneously. Complex characters are built by hidden connections between seeming contradictions (40).

---

*Or yell at them. There is a play by Peter Handke in which the actors verbally attack the audience. This is not alienation, either, although it is offensive. Handke's play is called, aptly, *Offending the Audience*.

†You see?

Analyzing Episodes: Rehearsing a Scene from *Richard III*

Shakespeare's use of episodes makes it possible for actors to build such complex characters by playing *roles* that revel in the contradictions of personality. The performer playing Lady Macbeth, for example, has the opportunity to juxtapose episodes of demonic possession with contradictory and intimate episodes of tenderness and fear. These oppositions build depth to the character of the murderous Lady Macbeth in the way contradictory episodes make Turgenev's mercurial Natalya Petrovna so charming. In more than one of Shakespeare's plays contradictions define the character: Hamlet, of course, but also Cleopatra, Iago, King Lear, Falstaff, Romeo, Juliet, and the crowd in *Julius Caesar*. Shakespeare's texts also provide good opportunities to examine *gests*, transactions, and episodes. Brecht studied them for structure and their implication for actors. So can you.

Let's organize the episodes of Shakespeare's *Richard III*, Act I, scene ii. In the course of the play, Richard of Gloster becomes sovereign the old-fashioned way: by killing anyone who stands in his way. On his way to the throne he stops to marry a politically well-connected widow, and tells the audience his plan before his scene with her begins. In many of his plays, Shakespeare wrote lines to explain action—before, during, and after the actor's performances of it. That's the case here:

> GLOSTER [RICHARD] . . . I'll marry Warwick's youngest daughter:
> What though I kill'd her husband and her father?
> The readiest way to make the wench amends
> Is to become her husband and her father . . .

Caption the episodes

As the next scene begins, Warwick's youngest daughter, better known as Lady Anne, enters, probably during the speech describing her. She accompanies her father-in-law's body on its way to burial. Her husband is also dead, murdered by Richard, Duke of Gloster, who intrudes on and interrupts the burial procession. Let's skip over Anne's monologue; the technique to be used for Shakespeare's monologues will be described—at length—in Chapter 13, "Shakespeare's Soliloquies." Even so, we can *caption* the first episode:

WIDOW ON WAY TO CEMETERY

The scene continues after the monologue. Lady Anne speaks to her gentlemen followers:

> ANNE . . . And still, as you are weary of the weight,
> Rest you, whiles I lament King Henry's corpse.

> *Enter* GLOSTER

GLOSTER Stay, you that bear the corpse, and set it down.
ANNE What black magician conjures up this fiend,
    To stop devoted charitable deeds?

Anne just announced the episode: *Fiend interrupts charitable deeds*. Richard himself told the audience he killed Anne's husband and father-in-law; from his own words and Anne's we know that Richard is unnaturally shaped. For the fun of it, let's caption the episode onstage in the style of tabloid newspapers:

DEFORMED KILLER CRASHES FUNERAL PROCESSION

GLOSTER Villains, set down the corpse; or, by Saint Paul,
    I'll make a corpse of him that disobeys.
GENTLEMAN My lord, stand back, and let the coffin pass.
GLOSTER Unmanner'd dog! stand thou, when I command:
    Advance thy halberd higher than my breast,
    Or, by Saint Paul, I'll strike thee to my foot,
    And spurn upon thee, beggar, for thy boldness.

This is the first transaction: *Put down the body / and I won't kill you*.

ANNE What, do you tremble? Are you all afraid?
    Alas, I blame you not; for you are mortal,
    And mortal eyes cannot endure the devil.

Based on what Anne describes, the Gentlemen, trembling and afraid (and so playing an opposition), accept the deal. The *gest* is the moment they lower their spears (halberds) from Richard's heart or put down the coffin as he has commanded. Clever directors and cleverer actors can polish the *gest* so it gleams:

Richard standing on top of the coffin, the spears of the guards pointed at him like a hunted boar. He swings his ax over the heads of Anne's guards, who lower the coffin submissively.

Or, if you don't trust the guards to lower the coffin smoothly:

Richard suddenly points his sword at the throat of the Gentleman. The guards, in fear, first lower their spears, then their eyes, then their heads. The loud clatter of the spears hitting the ground makes for a pause that alienates what follows.

The actress playing Anne will look at the *gest* while it happens, or turn her head away in fear and disgust, or in some other way *alienate* the moment for the audience—so that the public knows the moment is significant. What grief Anne might feel or exhibit should be focused on the event onstage. If she weeps so feelingly that we sympathize with her and lose the point of the scene, that's the same as if she sobbed so loudly we couldn't hear the other people's lines. Even if that is what the character would have done if she were a real person, *which she isn't*, every actor on stage should cooperate as part of an ensemble to perform the *gest*.

As the guards submit, we learn something about the social relations in the world of this play: even at a funeral, might makes right.

Choose opportunities for opposition

Richard can be gentle and soft while he threatens the guards: "It hurts me more than it hurts you to hold this sword to your trembling larynx." This would be one way to play the opposition, and it would be appropriately charming and witty. Snarling and hissing like a boar at bay might be better, though, since the next lines reveal that the playwright has another opposition in mind.

> ANNE Avaunt, thou dreadful minister of hell!
>   Thou hadst but power over his mortal body,
>   His soul thou canst not have; therefore, be gone.
> GLOSTER Sweet saint, for charity, be not so curst.

This is an opposition of Richard's roles from episode to episode—"unmannerly dog" with the lady's guards, "sweet saint" when speaking to the lady herself.

> ANNE Foul devil, for God's sake, hence, and trouble us not;
>   For thou hast made the happy earth thy hell,
>   Fill'd it with cursing cries and deep exclaims.
>   If thou delight to view thy heinous deeds,
>   Behold this pattern of thy butcheries.
>   O, gentlemen, see, see! dead Henry's wounds
>   Open their congeal'd mouths and bleed afresh!

It was a popular superstition in Shakespeare's day that a corpse would bleed in the presence of its killer. Richard killed Anne's husband, and also her father-in-law, whose corpse lies in front of her. The body bleeds in Richard's presence.

> ANNE Blush, Blush, thou lump of foul deformity;
>   For 'tis thy presence that exhales this blood
>   From cold and empty veins, where no blood dwells;
>   Thy deed, inhuman and unnatural,
>   Provokes this deluge most unnatural.
>   O God, which this blood mad'st, revenge his death!

There's a transaction here. She offers up the blood to God in exchange for righteous punishment. No deal. God doesn't respond. That's the next episode. Here's a caption:

NEITHER GOD NOR MAN PROTECTS THE WIDOW

> ANNE O earth, which this blood drink'st revenge his death!
>   Either heaven with lightning strike the murderer dead;
>   Or, earth, gape open wide and eat him quick,
>   As thou dost swallow up this good king's blood
>   Which his hell-govern'd arm hath butchered!

There needs to be a *gest* here, too. *Now* Anne can sob loudly, satisfied that everyone is watching her do so. Richard can smile, Anne can weep, the guards can pray. The audience can even sympathize, since they understand that, within the episode, Anne's tears are one side of an opposition that won't help her any more than the guards' prayers.

Identify the transactions

The next episode begins. We'll label it a little later, when we know a little more about its conclusion. It begins with an announcement:

> GLOSTER Lady, you know no rules of charity,
>   Which renders good for bad, blessings for curses.

Richard has just announced the transactions that will follow: "Good for bad, blessings for curses"—*If you call me Saint / I'll call you Devil*.

The line itself can be split. The first part, "Lady, you know no rules of charity" can be said to Lady Anne. But, if you like, "Which renders good for bad, blessings for curses" can be spoken directly to the audience. This report to the audience is not a melodramatic whispered aside. The information is declared at full volume so that the audience watching Gloster and Anne can savor the exchanges that will follow. The actress playing Anne doesn't have to stand there and pretend she doesn't hear this report to the audience. She can respond from Anne's point of view about Richard's rending "blessings for curses."

> ANNE Villain, thou know'st no law of God nor man:
>   No beast so fierce but knows some touch of pity.
> GLOSTER But I know none, and therefore am no beast.

And if the actress playing Anne wishes to, she can make her *own* report to the audience:

> ANNE O wonderful, when devils tell the truth!

The two can vie for the audience's understanding:

> GLOSTER More wonderful, when angels are so angry.

PLAYING EPISODES

And Richard can return to speaking to Anne:

> GLOSTER Vouchsafe, divine perfection of a woman,
>   Of these supposed evils to give me leave,
>   By circumstance, but to acquit myself.
> ANNE Vouchsafe, defus'd infection of a man,
>   For these known evils but to give me leave,
>   By circumstance, to curse thy cursed self.

The pattern of the transaction is for every curse he'll give her a blessing—perfection for infection, fair for foul, angel for devil. There are more:

> GLOSTER Fairer than tongue can name thee, let me have
>   Some patient leisure to excuse myself.
> ANNE Fouler than heart can think thee, thou canst make
>   No excuse current, but to hang thyself.
> GLOSTER By such despair, I should accuse myself.
> ANNE And, by despairing, shouldst thou stand excused;
>   For doing worthy vengeance on thyself,
>   Which didst unworthy slaughter upon others.
> GLOSTER Say that I slew them not?
> ANNE Then say they were not slain:
>   But dead they are, and devilish slave, by thee.
> GLOSTER I did not kill your husband.
> ANNE Why, then he is alive.
> GLOSTER Nay, he is dead; and slain by Edward's hand.

Another transaction is happening here, as Richard offers Anne his version of her husband's death.

> ANNE In thy foul throat thou liest:

She doesn't seem to be buying this history.

> ANNE Queen Margaret saw
>   Thy murderous falchion smoking in his blood;
>   The which thou once didst bend against her breast,
>   But that thy brothers beat aside the point.
> GLOSTER I was provoked by her slanderous tongue,
>   That laid their guilt upon my guiltless shoulders.
> ANNE Thou wast provoked by thy bloody mind.
>   Which never dreamt on aught but butcheries:
>   Didst thou not kill this king?
> GLOSTER I grant ye.

Okay, he'll buy her version. What will Richard want her to grant him in exchange?

> ANNE Dost grant me, hedgehog? then, God grant me too
>   Thou mayst be damned for that wicked deed!
>   O, he was gentle, mild, and virtuous!
> GLOSTER The fitter for the King of heaven, that hath him.
> ANNE He is in heaven, where thou shalt never come.
> GLOSTER Let him thank me, that holp to send him thither;
>   For he was fitter for that place than earth.
> ANNE And thou unfit for any place but hell.
> GLOSTER Yes, one place else, if you will hear me name it.
> ANNE Some dungeon.
> GLOSTER Your bed-chamber.

Here is the essential transaction of the scene. Notice how the playwright helps to alienate the moment by changing the rhythm of the verse. Several overlong lines with twelve or eleven beats—not just the familiar ten—precede two short lines of three and four beats: *some' dun'geon / your bed'—cham'ber.* If you'd like to further admire Shakespeare's technique, notice how the vowels of *some, dun, geon,* and *your* precede the very different sound of *bed*.

The episode is obvious now. If tabloids had been around in the 1480s, they might have read:

KILLER HUNCHBACK PITCHES WOO TO VICTIM'S WIDOW

> ANNE I'll rest betide the chamber where thou liest!
> GLOSTER So will it, madam till I lie with you.
> ANNE I hope so.
> GLOSTER I know so. But, gentle Lady Anne,
>   To leave this keen encounter of our wits,
>   And fall somewhat into a slower method,

The announced change to a slower tempo alienates the lines that follow. But first, there comes another report to the audience, or rather, a question.

> GLOSTER Is not the causer of the timeless deaths
>   Of these Plantagenets, Henry and Edward,
>   As blameful as the executioner?

Anne supplies her own answer.

> ANNE Thou wast the cause, and most accurs'd effect.
> GLOSTER Your beauty was the cause of that effect;
>   Your beauty, that did haunt me in my sleep

> To undertake the death of all the world,
> So I might live one hour in your sweet bosom.

The beauty of these lines, alienated by the change in tempo, is meant to be understood as part of an opposition in which the cold-blooded killer speaks rapturous verse.

Notice that Richard is creating a *role* for Anne as his sweetheart. A woman cast as darling to the man whom she hates is, yes, another opposition. The weirdness of the scene is that, say what she will, do what she wants, Anne finds herself playing a love scene. There are at least two personae so far for each of the roles. Richard: Lying Killer and Poetic Lover. Anne: Good Faithful Widow and Poet's Beloved.

> ANNE If I thought that, I tell thee, homicide,
>   These nails should rend that beauty from my cheeks.
> GLOSTER These eyes could not endure sweet beauty's wreck;
>   You should not blemish it, if I stood by:
>   As all the world is cheer'd by the sun,
>   So I by that; it is my day, my life.
> ANNE Black night o'ershade thy day, and death thy life!
> GLOSTER Curse not thyself, fair creature thou art both.
> ANNE I would I were, to be reveng'd on thee.
> GLOSTER It is a quarrel most unnatural,
>   To be reveng'd on him that loveth thee.

That loveth thee! That's the full offer. He offers her his love. Perhaps in exchange for her life?

> ANNE It is a quarrel just and reasonable,
>   To be reveng'd on him that killed my husband.
> GLOSTER He that bereft thee, lady, of thy husband,
>   Did it to help thee to a better husband.
> ANNE His better doth not breathe upon the earth.
> GLOSTER He lives that loves thee better than he could.
> ANNE Name him.
> GLOSTER Plantagenet.

Richard and the men he killed come from the same family, Plantagenet. Offering himself to Anne as a Plantagenet is Richard's deceptive advertising for a contract with a lot of other hidden clauses.

> ANNE Why, that was he.
> GLOSTER The self-same name, but one of better nature.
> ANNE Where is he?
> GLOSTER Here.

He offers himself. A stage direction is included: *she spits at him*. This certainly could be a *gest*. Does Anne hesitate before spitting? Does she do it impulsively? Does Richard wipe it off, let it hang on his face? Lick it as if it were delicious?

> GLOSTER Why dost thou spit at me?
> ANNE Would it were mortal poison, for thy sake!
> GLOSTER: Never came poison from so sweet a place.
> ANNE Never hung poison on a fouler toad.
>   Out of my sight! thou dost infect mine eyes.
> GLOSTER Thine eyes, sweet lady, have infected mine.
> ANNE Would they were basilisks, to strike thee dead!

Basilisks were mythological animals that killed their prey by staring at them. Notice that another transaction is taking place: *If you'll behave like a toad / I'll behave like a basilisk.*

> GLOSTER I would they were, that I might die at once;
>   For now they kill me with a living death.
>   Those eyes of thine from mine have drawn salt tears,
>   Shamed their aspect with store of childish drops;

She gives him spit, he will give her tears; valuable tears at that, as he points out to her:

> GLOSTER These eyes, which never shed remorseful tear,

His tears are rare. Richard never cries—not even at the story of his father's death.

> GLOSTER No, when my father York and Edward wept,
>   To hear the piteous moan that Rutland made
>   When black-faced Clifford shook his sword at him;
>   Nor when thy warlike father, like a child,
>   Told the sad story of my father's death,
>   And twenty times made pause, to sob and weep,
>   That all the standers-by had wet their cheeks,
>   Like trees bedash'd with rain: in that sad time
>   My manly eyes did scorn an humble tear;
>   And what these sorrows could not thence exhale,
>   Thy beauty hath, and made them blind with weeping.

How shall the actor playing Richard do this? By isolating the episode, playing it by itself. Don't manipulate Anne. Don't try to persuade her. Act out the caption:

THE HARDENED KILLER WEEPS

The sight of an actor working up his tears—and calling the audience's attention to his craft in doing so—is quite useful for this episode. In this way and others, Richard's tears are alienated.

GLOSTER I never sued to friend nor enemy;
 My tongue could never learn sweet smoothing word;
 But, now thy beauty is propos'd my fee,
 My proud heart sues, and prompts my tongue to speak.

Another episode is happening here, but it's not one you could necessarily derive from the lines. Once again, for the purposes of analysis we are reversing the usual process of taking notes after the rehearsal. But imagine what is happening onstage. In rehearsal, the episode would be obvious:

WIDOW HEARS THE MURDERER OUT

That Anne stops and does not leave while her husband's murderer speaks at length is a significant onstage event. Why does she do it? It doesn't matter. She does it, and that's enough for you to establish. Let the ladies in the balcony argue why. The opposition Anne can play during this episode is that while Richard is weeping, Anne can be listening critically and yet—against her will—be moved.

 The transaction proposed here is that Anne buy Richard's tears in exchange for her sympathy. Her response to the offer is announced by a stage direction:

She looks scornfully at him.

GLOSTER Teach not thy lips such scorn, for they were made
 For kissing, lady, not for such contempt.
 If thy revengeful heart cannot forgive,
 Lo, here I lend thee this sharp-pointed sword;
 Which if thou please to hide in this true breast
 And let the soul forth that adoreth thee,
 I lay it naked to the deadly stroke,
 And humbly beg the death upon my knee.

He lays his breast open: she offers at it with his sword.

A new caption—HE OFFERS HER HIS LIFE—and with it a new transaction: *You may kill me / but you must accept that you are guilty too.*

GLOSTER Nay, do not pause; for I did kill King Henry,
 But 'twas thy beauty that provoked me.

Anne is unable to pay the price.

GLOSTER Nay, now dispatch; 'twas I that stabb'd young Edward,
 But 'twas thy heavenly face that set me on.

COMBINING EPISODES

Here Anne lets fall the sword. This, too, is a *gest*. The transaction is stated openly now:

> GLOSTER Take up the sword again, or take up me.
> ANNE Arise, dissembler: though I wish thy death,
>   I will not be thy executioner.

Gloster rising is another alienated moment. Anne tries to wriggle out of the deal, but we in the audience know that by dropping the sword she is taking up her husband's killer. Reluctant to pay the price of killing Richard (the mess, the sin, the scandal!), she's accepted his other offer. The proud warrior, rising in front of his lady love, is the meaning of the *gest*—whether Anne likes it or not.

If you consider the scene separately from the *emotions* of the individual roles, and concentrate on what the roles *do* despite their "feelings" (or lack of feelings), another episode can be understood and made clear to the audience. Anne is the Good Faithful Widow, Richard is the Lying Killer. Playing her role of Good Faithful Widow, Anne will not commit the sin of murder, and she will behave according to this role during what follows, even offering her goodness and faith toward a miserable liar—in exchange for more misery and lies. A possible line of interpretation, then, is to label the next episode ANNE EXTENDS HER FAITH TO THE FAITHLESS. Playing this episode, Anne will maintain not just her role as Good Faithful Widow, but also the role Richard has cast her in: his Beloved.

Anne may act on the premise *it is a sin to kill, it is a sin not to forgive*, but the audience does not have to limit their understanding to Anne's understanding. Although the actors will not establish cause and effect as a way to connect this episode with episodes that follow (episodes in which Richard orders the death of children and happily slaughters innocent men), the audience will be able to witness the progression and make up their own minds about the sequence that leads from the personal (her grief, his ambition), to the "larger" and more "political" aspect of the entire scene, which might have as its caption THINKING TO DO GOOD, THE GOOD PROMOTE EVIL.

At this point in the progression, the smaller episode can be labeled ANNE EXTENDS HER FAITH TO THE FAITHLESS. The finer points of their contract follow over the stated offer: *take up the sword / or take up me.*

> GLOSTER Then bid me kill myself, and I will do it.
> ANNE I have already.
> GLOSTER Tush, that was in thy rage:
>   Speak it again, and, even with the word,
>   This hand, which for thy love did kill thy love,
>   Shall, for thy love, kill a far truer love;
>   To both their deaths shalt thou be accessory.

In order to better get the sense of this as sales pitch, say it out loud and see where the natural emphasis of the rhythm of the verse hits.

> Speak it again, and, even with the word,
> This hand, which for thy LOVE did kill thy LOVE,

Shall, for thy LOVE, kill a far truer LOVE;
To both their deaths shalt thou be accessory.

Anne now begins to haggle over details of the offer she accepted when she allowed Richard to rise. Within the episode of ANNE EXTENDS HER FAITH TO THE FAITHLESS, Anne weighs Gloster's offer of love:

> ANNE I would I knew thy heart.
> GLOSTER 'Tis figured in my tongue.
> ANNE I fear me both are false.
> GLOSTER Then never man was true.
> ANNE Well, well, put up your sword.
> GLOSTER Say, then, my peace is made.
> ANNE That shall you know hereafter.
> GLOSTER But shall I live in hope?
> ANNE All men, I hope, live so.

The back-and-forth haggling here includes his tongue for her heart, her truth for his truth, his pursuit in exchange for her evasion, and a bargain proposing that Richard's act of putting away his sword be done in exchange for Anne's words of acceptance—or, better yet, her *public* act of acceptance.

> GLOSTER Vouchsafe to wear this ring.
> ANNE To take is not to give.

Anne saying "to take is not to give" could be an episode in itself: ANNE AGREES WITHOUT UNDERSTANDING THE PRICE.

> *She puts on the ring.*

> GLOSTER Look, how this ring encompasseth finger.
> Even so thy breast encloseth my poor heart;
> Wear both of them, for both of them are thine.

The entire scene now seems to be organized around one episode. There is not one interpretation, but several: HUNCHBACK ADVANCES FROM DESPISED KILLER TO LOVER or ANNE AGREES WITHOUT UNDERSTANDING THE PRICE or THINKING TO DO GOOD, THE WIDOW PROMOTES EVIL.

Polish the *gest*

How does Anne receive the ring? Is there a smile on her face? A gleam in her eye? A catch in her throat? Is her head bent away from Richard, even as her hand reaches out to him—an opposition? Does he take her hand in his? Does she slip the ring on herself? Does she shiver as she does it?

From where does Richard get the ring? His own finger? How carefully, quickly, readily does he slip it off? Are his hands clean? Does he treat the ring as if it were valuable? Does he hold it up in the air for the audience to see it sparkle? Does he hold it up in the air so that *Anne* may see it sparkle? Does he drop it? Does he thoughtfully hand it to her in a cloth so her hand doesn't need to touch his? As Anne's hand reaches out for the ring, does Richard playfully snatch it back, alienating her gesture of reaching out to him? Perhaps the guards smile as Anne reaches out for the ring. This, too, would alienate her outstretched hand—and Richard could then play an opposition, deadly serious and disapproving in what should be for him a moment of pleasure.

The rehearsal process of testing, trying, and perfecting these nuances can be thought of as *polishing the gest*. As with forks, so with rehearsals: once polished, the *gest* should gleam, burnished with use and care. *Gests* are not shaped by the internal desire of the characters who perform them; they are physical activities that require an actor's skill, forethought, and practice. They clarify the episode, so that even though Anne says, "to take is not to give," an audience watching the *gest* knows better.

This *gest* of Anne receiving Richard's ring has the potential to alienate a familiar transaction: how once-powerful women accept the favors of unpleasant-but-powerful men. Could the wedding of Jacqueline Kennedy to Aristotle Onassis give you some ideas? He handed her the ring on a pillow. Why? Let the ladies in the balcony argue over the *why*; it's more than enough to present the *how*.

Review the tableaux

You should be able to confirm the episode by comparing the beginning tableau with the ultimate tableau. In this scene, the *gests* resemble photographs in a tabloid: *Richard interrupting the funeral procession. Richard slipping the ring on Anne's finger.* Shakespeare was so concerned that the audience understand what happened in this scene that Richard announces the caption of the episode before the action begins—"I'll marry Warwick's youngest daughter"—and repeats the caption after the episode is complete:

> GLOSTER Was ever woman in this humor wooed?
>   Was ever woman in this humor won?

Let's Review Terms

opposition	contradictions, simultaneous or sequential, deliberately included in a performance in order to create a dynamic fusion of opposing forces
alienation	making the familiar seem strange—or alien—by taking what is familiar out of context

Notebook: Combining Episodes

GLOSTER Why dost thou spit at me?

ANNE Would it were mortal poison, for thy sake!

GLOSTER Never came poison from so sweet a place.

ANNE Never hung poison on a fouler toad.
　　　　Out of my sight! thou dost infect mine eyes.

GLOSTER Thine eyes, sweet lady, have infected
　　　　mine.

ANNE Would they were basilisks, to strike thee
　　　　dead!

GLOSTER I would they were, that I might die at
　　　　once;
　　　　For now they kill me with a living death.
　　　　Those eyes of thine from mine have drawn
　　　　　　salt tears,
　　　　Shamed their aspects with store of childish
　　　　　　drops;
　　　　These eyes, which never shed remorseful
　　　　　　tear,
　　　　No, when my father York and Edward wept,
　　　　To hear the piteous moan that Rutland made
　　　　When black-faced Clifford shook his sword
　　　　　　at him;
　　　　Nor when thy warlike father, like a child,
　　　　Told the sad story of my father's death,
　　　　And twenty times made pause, to sob and
　　　　　　weep,
　　　　That all the standers-by had wet their cheeks,
　　　　Like trees bedash'd with rain: in that sad time
　　　　My manly eyes did scorn an humble tear;
　　　　And what these sorrows could not thence
　　　　　　exhale,
　　　　Thy beauty hath, and made them blind
　　　　　　with weeping.
　　　　I never sued to friend nor enemy;
　　　　My tongue could never learn sweet
　　　　　　smoothing word;
　　　　But, now thy beauty is propos'd my fee,
　　　　My proud heart sues, and prompts my
　　　　　　tongue to speak.

EPISODE: KILLER HUNCHBACK PITCHES WOO TO VICTIM'S WIDOW
Richard's role: The Poetic Lover
Anne's role: The Beloved
Transaction offered: *his body*

gest: She spits at him
(his offer rejected)

Transactions:
toad / sweet
infection / affection
love / spit
spit / tears

EPISODE: THE HARDENED KILLER WEEPS
Transaction offered:
his tears / for her sympathy

Alienation: the tears are rare

Opposition:
Despite herself, Anne is moved

gest: She turns her head away
so he can't see her reaction

EPISODE: WIDOW HEARS KILLER OUT
Transaction offered:
his word / for her acceptance

Opposition: The beauty of his speech,
the ugliness of his body and mind

Opposition: Her wanting to be kind to
the cruel

COMBINING EPISODES

She looks scornfully at him.

GLOSTER Teach not thy lips such scorn, for they
      were made
    For kissing, lady, not for such contempt.
    If thy revengeful heart cannot forgive,
    Lo, here I lend thee this sharp-pointed
      sword;
    Which if thou please to hide in this true
      breast.
    And let the soul forth that adoreth thee,
    I lay it naked to the deadly stroke,
    And humbly beg the death upon my knee.

He lays his breast open:
she offers at (it} with his sword.

GLOSTER Nay, do not pause; for I did kill King
      Henry,
    But 'twas thy beauty that provoked me.
    Nay, now dispatch; 'twas I that stabb'd
      young Edward,
    But 'twas thy heavenly face that set me on.
               She lets fall the sword.
GLOSTER <u>Take up the sword again, or take up me.</u>

ANNE Arise, dissembler: though I wish thy death,
    I will not be thy executioner.
GLOSTER Then bid me kill myself, and I will do it.
ANNE I have already.
GLOSTER Tush, that was in thy rage:
    Speak it again, and, even with the word,
    This hand, which for thy love did kill thy
      love,
    Shall, for thy love, kill a far truer love;
    To both their deaths shalt thou be accessory.

Offer rejected:
She looks scornfully at him

EPISODE: HE OFFER HER HIS LIFE
Transaction offered:
You may kill me / the cost is hidden

gest?: He gets down on
his knees and bares his breast

EPISODE: ANNE CAN'T BRING
HERSELF TO KILL HIM
Transaction offered:
*You may kill me / but you must accept
that you are guilty too*

Offer rejected:
gest. Her hand shaking, but not
reaching the sword or *gest:* He rises

EPISODE: ANNE EXTENDS HER
FAITH TO THE FAITHLESS
Transaction offered:
<u>*Take up the sword again /*</u>
<u>*or take up me.*</u>

Transaction offered:
*to replace her old husband /
with a new husband (himself!)*

ANNE I would I knew thy heart.

GLOSTER 'Tis figured in my tongue.

ANNE I fear me both are false.

GLOSTER Then never man was true.

ANNE Well, well, put up your sword.

GLOSTER Say, then, my peace is made.

ANNE That shall you know hereafter.

GLOSTER But shall I live in hope?

ANNE All men, I hope, live so.

GLOSTER Vouchsafe to wear this ring.

ANNE <u>To take is not to give.</u>

She puts on the ring.

GLOSTER Look, how this ring encompasseth thy
      finger.
      Even so thy breast encloseth my poor heart;
      Wear both of them, for both of them are
      thine.

Transactions:
heart / tongue
true / false
her evasion / his pursuit
his act / her words:
he'll put away his sword /
she'll say for all to hear that they're at
peace

EPISODE: ANNE AGREES
WITHOUT UNDERSTANDING THE PRICE
<u>To take is not to give</u>

Offer accepted:
<u>She puts on the ring</u>
gest: Richard slipping the ring on
Anne's finger

Alienation?: He drops the ring, she
reaches for it with a reflex action, the
watching guards smile

Opposition?: Richard is annoyed that
the ring fell and that the guards smile

EPISODE:
HUNCHBACK ADVANCES FROM
DESPISED KILLER TO LOVER
or
ANNE SIGNS A CONTRACT
UNAWARE OF THE PRICE
or
THINKING TO DO GOOD,
THE WIDOW DOES EVIL

Practical Tips for Working

Watch each other

Gests and episodes are aimed at the audience; it's helpful to sit in the audience yourself. If the director will allow you, ask another actor to imitate what you do in a scene. Watch someone else perform your *gest* and learn how effectively it communicates to an audience. You might ask other actors to perform your *gest* their own way and then, like Brecht, help yourself to their ideas.* If you have an understudy, or are doubling a role, watch while the other person rehearses. If you can't get off the stage to get some distance, still try to be aware of the stage picture and what other people are doing around you. These things help to define your role.

Share ideas

Episodic work is collaborative. The people performing an episode need to work together for the same reason machine parts should fit together. This happens more often than you think; learn to pay attention when it does. In the course of rehearsal, a caption will be agreed on informally even if the other actors don't have the will or the vocabulary to discuss a scene in this manner. When someone says, "Let's rehearse the scene where she takes the ring," the caption is being announced for all to understand and agree on. You can start the ball rolling by mentioning your own idea of what happens in the scene to see if anyone else agrees or disagrees with you. It's strategic to put it in the form of a question: *You mean the scene where she practically marries him, right?*

Read the stage directions aloud

Anne has a stage direction to perform: *she spits at him.* Read it aloud at first, rather than acting it out. Understand the transaction and its role in the episode before you work up that saliva. Another useful technique is to say aloud *Anne says* or *I say* before repeating your lines. This alienates the words in rehearsal so that you can examine what is going on in the scene before you take on the responsibility of animating your role with a feeling or a point of view. In his rehearsals, Brecht sometimes had actors insert *I say* or *she says* in the middle of lines in order to alienate overly familiar speech rhythms.

Stage the tableaux first (or imagine them)

When the action of a scene baffles you, try to imagine what the audience would see when the scene begins, and what they would see when the scene ends. What *changes* between the two tableaux? A ring on your finger? How it got there is probably the episode. The moment when it changes is probably the *gest*. A director might choose to stage

---

*A common Brechtian device.

.

41

tableaux first before further work on the action of the scene. Even if that doesn't happen, you can picture the tableaux for yourself. Here's a clue for an episode: You enter the room perky and ready for a lesson; by the end of the scene you're carried out dead.

Enjoy the freedom from relentless realism

Realism is one among many styles. Experiment with others. Smash the fourth wall. Worry about externals like posture and diction. Break the illusion of character. Comment on what you're doing. Try alternate ways in rehearsal to *demonstrate* the episode, rather than enact it. Look for inconsistencies as a way to play an opposition. Use direct, even crude ways to get the episode across. You can find more subtle methods later. Expand your ideas of good taste. You can't *be* refined until you have something *to* refine.

Avoid the temptation to include motivation

It's a proud habit of many actors to include motivation in any episode, but it's not always necessary for understanding an episode, nor does it always add anything to the performance. By solving the riddle of *why*, you limit the chance the audience has to provide their own explanation—or enjoy the paradox of inexplicable behavior. Think of it this way: in an episodic performance, you provide the recipe but the audience bakes the cake—and then they complete the experience by eating and digesting the cake at home.*

Avoid the temptation to undermine episodic work with a super-task that dulls the contradictions of a role. Avoid sabotaging your ability to perform an episode by itself by hunting for what cannot be found—like Olga Knipper in her fruitless pursuit for the sources of Natalya Petrovna's whims. If you're playing Lady Anne in *Richard III* you can waste a lot of time in rehearsal trying to motivate that ring scene. *Why* does she do it? Spare yourself and others the question—it isn't your business to answer it.

Think beyond the personal

Just as you sat in the audience to watch what your role did in the context of the stage picture, try to get some distance in your thinking from the emotions of your role in the context of the episode. If the episode for the Lady Anne scene is THINKING TO DO GOOD, THE WIDOW PROMOTES EVIL, you'll need to think about the scene from a point of view other than Anne's. Revealing this aspect of the scene to yourself allows you to reveal it to the director in rehearsal, and to the audience in performance. Brecht and Piscator wanted their actors to make a habit of this awareness and use it actively to eradicate the impulse toward compassion for a role (a compassion Stanislavsky prized highly). Such awareness can be just as deeply felt as compassion. You could call it "political awareness"—Brecht and Piscator would have liked that—but you don't have to.

---

*Brecht allegedly made the charmless comment that if the actors themselves ate and digested the performance as if it were a meal, what was next presented to the audience might be better left in the toilet.

Write a letter to your grandmother

A good way to begin to analyze an episode is to describe what you are doing onstage in a letter to your grandmother, who isn't able to attend the performance:

> Dear Grandma,
> I am in a play. In the first scene I'm minding my own business, quietly working in a library, when a strange man comes in and picks a fight with me.

This kind of direct report of what you *do* while performing a role is what Brecht meant in his example of good acting (remember the actor teaching the role of Hamlet to his understudy?). PS: It's a good idea to write your grandmother anyway.

The Resemblance to Posters

A poster makes a good model for structuring a performance into episodes. Like an actor performing an episode, a poster should relay its information directly and clearly, using whatever means—graphics, pictures, text, layout, color, anything that can be printed on the paper. A poster has to be eye-catching. It has to be understandable to people, no matter who they are. It also has to be understandable to people no matter where the poster is posted: on one wall or another, by itself, or next to two other posters.

Just so, an episode needs to be understood by everyone, by itself, outside of its sequence.

Like actors playing an episode, a poster is meant to tell something, sell something, or, at the very least, relay an idea. Yes, a poster can have an aesthetic appeal. You wouldn't want an ugly or a dull one. But the aesthetic of a poster is different from the aesthetic of a realistic nineteenth-century painting in which artists placed oil glazes onto canvas, layer over layer, in order to create the illusion of depth. A poster maker can accomplish the illusion of depth by overlapping flat shapes. Episodic acting is similarly graphic and direct. It can include the nuances of depth and shading or it can dispense with them and still make its point.

The Chart

Let's return to the chart. Under the column of *Episodic Analysis* there are still some categories to be filled in.

- **Unifying image.** The unifying image is the direct graphic design of a *poster*.
- **The intended reaction of the audience.** Episodic acting encourages the audience to synthesize a story from the progression of episodes. Brecht wanted his audience *to sit in judgment of the action.*

- **The illusion of character.** *Playing the opposition* of roles is the way an actor creates the illusion of depth in character, while organizing a performance episodically.
- **Suitable playwrights.** All plays need to be clear to their audience, and in that sense all plays are suitable for episodic analysis. Some writers wrote using episodic structure, and their work is particularly appropriate for this technique: among many others, *Shakespeare, Samuel Beckett, Gertrude Stein, Harold Pinter, Caryl Churchill*, medieval playwrights, and, of course, *Bertolt Brecht*.
- **The relative theory.** *Marxism* parallels Brecht's elaboration of episodic acting, just as Freud's ideas parallel Stanislavsky's ideas of motivation. This requires some comment and elaboration before we rig up the fig leaf of an alternative theory of transactions and roles: the *psychology of transactions*.

The Social(ist) Context

Brecht's idea of acting—that behavior is commerce—borrows Karl Marx's interpretation of history as an economic process. For Marx and for Brecht, human interaction is a series of transactions: sales, trades, buy-outs, or the collapse of a deal. The idea of oppositions is also part of Marxist thinking studied by Brecht. For some people, the association of Brecht's ideas with the history of Communism has discredited their use in the theater.

The limitations of Marx

Since 1989, when the Berlin Wall fell, life under the Communist system has become the study of coprophiliacs (look it up in a good dictionary!), not actors. On the pettiest level, nobody who has spent time in Soviet countries with open eyes and a working nose can have anything too nice to say about the Communist system. No one who has experienced an entire city being routinely deprived of hot water for a month—because the hot water comes from a central communal supply—can defend the Communist system as a workable idea. When Brecht was asked why he didn't stay in Moscow after 1935, he said it was because he couldn't get sugar for his tea. He wasn't kidding.

Still, a condemnation of the Communist system does not toss out all Communist ideas any more than a child-molesting priest (or ten child-molesting priests or one hundred child-molesting priests) discredits the Christian idea of compassion or the Catholic concept of Grace. It is undeniable that the skills of cooperation should be studied, practiced, and encouraged just as much if not more than the instinct for competition and self-preservation. True, the Communist use of cooperation included cooperative murder—but then the Borgia Popes had their own scurrilous uses for the gracious Sistine Chapel, freshly decorated by Michelangelo.

Brecht prepared a parable to illustrate his own choice between Capitalism and Communism (as if those were the only options!): he was like a doctor with limited resources selecting which patient to assist—an old lecher with terminal cancer (Capitalism), or a pregnant syphilitic whore (Communism). The doctor's sympathies were with the whore. Brecht's sympathies would be with the whore for any number of reasons, but in this case it was principally because she was pregnant with hope for the future.

That's a very nice explanation, and a very good example of the smooth way that Brecht, a Communist apologist, could rationalize the system that deliberately starved to death ten million Ukrainians. Even as he was aware that Stalin's atrocities persisted, Brecht accepted a Stalin Peace Prize. The ability to hold such irreconcilable truths simultaneously is a very good example of opposition. Here's another: To the consternation of the East German authorities, Brecht put most of the prize money in a Swiss bank.

Yet, the relationship that thinking people can be expected to have to the *history* of Communism (repugnance) is not at all the relationship they can be expected to have to Brecht's ideas about *acting*—or his so-far unreachable political ideals. Brecht offers open-minded people a powerful and compassionate understanding of human behavior: that it is necessary to reform the social system to realize a person's potential. Stanislavsky, Freud, and the Protestant work ethic may place responsibility on individuals for their lives. Brecht and the generation shell-shocked by the First World War could not agree. Soldiers didn't die because they lacked enthusiasm. The poor weren't hard-up because they lacked faith, conviction, or moral standards. They were part of a bargain with the rest of society that they did not understand and could not negotiate.

As a society and as individuals, we all enter into contracts we don't recognize, yet these transactions determine our lives. That's why you might pay attention to Brecht's ideas, whatever their source. For actors, Brecht's interpretation of human behavior is applicable to rehearsal, performance, and life.

Transactional analysis

The theories of the Viennese psychologist Alfred Adler also provide a model for interpreting behavior as transactions. If it makes you feel better, you can think of transactions as Adlerian, rather than Marxist. Adler claimed that behavior has an underlying structure of barter, rather than the satisfaction of desire, as Freud and Stanislavsky would have it. According to Adler, when people meet they subconsciously assess each other and unconsciously assume mutually dependent roles. People learn roles from family and society. There, the healthy instinct for conflict between roles is reconciled by unspoken contracts that organize a mediating series of transactions. An example of a transaction agreed on by most children: *I won't shout in order to get what I want, as long as you pay attention to me.*

Adler was trained as a medical doctor and began to counsel patients in 1898, the year that Brecht was born. Adler's first clients were the tailors, acrobats, and clowns who lived in the fairground district of Vienna dominated by a Ferris wheel. Adler saw how the hard-working people he cared for were suffering from work-related diseases, both psychological and physical, and his eyes were opened to the ways in which environment, family habits, and inadequate health care caused depression and other psychological states—just as much as, if not more than, Freud's theories of repressed desire.

Adler's wife, Raissa Epstein, a forthright Russian feminist, further opened Adler's eyes to the ways in which women's behavior and mental health were affected by women's social positions. Through his wife, Adler became a personal friend of the Communist revolutionary Leon Trotsky (they played chess and took their children to the park together). Adler wrote an early paper about the psychology of Marxism. *Cooperation* became one of the keystones of his thinking—how, for example, an infant cooperates with its mother in order to be breast-fed.

Adler's ultimate rejection of the Soviet system and of Stalin's perversion of cooperation were based on first-hand knowledge: his eldest child Valentine and her husband were arrested by Stalin's secret police and disappeared, possibly because of Adler and Epstein's friendship with Trotsky. Adler's opportunities for observation, then, differed from those of Freud, who—besides having had different clients, different friends, and a much more subservient wife—had a daughter, Anna, who grew up to continue her father's life work.*

Like those who map new lands, psychological explorers are given scope by what they encounter in their lives. The same is true for the twentieth-century explorers of episodic acting, whose personal histories shaped how episodic acting was passed on, recorded, hidden—and reviled.

---

*In 1937, on the day before he died, Adler wrote his wife that he planned to go to Moscow himself to find out what had happened to Valentine. In 1945, Albert Einstein, whom Adler claimed as a follower, discovered that Valentine Adler had died in a Siberian gulag in 1942.

CHAPTER 3

THREE LIVES IN THE EPISODIC THEATER

Meyerhold in Russia

The course of three lives influenced the development of episodic acting in the twentieth century. In Germany, there were Bertolt Brecht and Erwin Piscator. In Russia, there was the great innovator Vsevolod Meyerhold, who, coincidentally, was from a German vodka-manufacturing family living in the little town of Penza, 350 miles south of Moscow. A founding member of MXAT, Meyerhold worked as an actor for Stanislavsky and was adept enough to play the central role of the young playwright Treplev in the company's landmark production of Chekhov's *Seagull*. Three years later Meyerhold created the role of the perversely contentious Baron Tuzenbach in the MXAT production of Chekhov's *Three Sisters*.

Stanislavsky recognized his protégé's brilliance early on. In 1905, after the failure of the MXAT *Julius Caesar* and other attempts at staging non-realistic texts, Stanislavsky invited Meyerhold to establish a studio in the new theater Stanislavsky was establishing outside of the Moscow Art Theater. The hope was to discover an approach to acting that would be suitable for non-realistic plays. To Stanislavsky's horror, Meyerhold, claiming to be "extending" his teacher's work, brought back external techniques Stanislavsky had spent his entire life up to then removing from the Russian stage. Stanislavsky even interrupted Meyerhold's last dress rehearsal because the lights weren't bright enough to see the actors' faces. *It goes against psychology!* cried out the Master.

Meyerhold's studio never resumed; its interruption was made permanent by the start of the first Russian revolution. Meyerhold embraced the revolt from its beginning. He became an active member of the Communist party, created plays with and for Bolshevik soldiers, and announced proudly that a new style of politically aimed acting would re-form modern man. Once the fighting subsided, Stanislavsky offered Meyerhold his old role of Treplev in the 1920 revival of *The Seagull*. Meyerhold declined. He was now more interested in directing and teaching acting than in being an actor himself.

Meyerhold searched for historical models for non-motivated acting. He studied and adapted the style and tricks of acrobats and clowns. He looked at the conventions of the ancient Greek theater, the physical craft of the Italian commedia dell'arte, and he analyzed how Shakespeare constructed dialogue, characters, and events without the formula of realism.

PLAYING EPISODES

At first Meyerhold called his work *constructivist theater*, naming it after an art movement of the time, *constructivism*. In constructivism, sculptures were constructed, like eccentric machines, from bits and pieces of other artwork and found objects. In a like manner, Meyerhold was piecing together parts of other theatrical systems. As part of his experiments, Meyerhold placed performers in the audience to explain what was happening onstage, he hung banners over the stage to caption scenes, he turned realistic dialogue into direct address to the public. He urged actors to break their performances into small units. The scenery and props of performances became tools to perform events, not illustrations of time and place.

With these and other innovative techniques, Meyerhold explored episodic acting a good twenty years before Brecht and Piscator. The word *episode*, which is Greek, passed directly into Russian. It recurs throughout Meyerhold's comments to his actors and students, peppers his essays, organizes his preparation notes, and studs his publicity announcements. For Meyerhold, structuring a play into episodes was essential to his work as a director working with actors.

As early as 1904 (when Brecht was six years old), Meyerhold noticed the phenomenon of opposition as an alternative to psychology in the theater. He wrote in an essay:

> It is natural that the rhythmical construction of a play like *Julius Caesar* with
> its precisely balanced conflict of two opposing forces is completely overlooked
> and so not even suggested [in the naturalistic theater] . . . (41)

Meyerhold's experiments with what Brecht would later call *gests* evolved from heightened physical interaction between characters at significant moments in an episode. These were codified in a set of movements called *biomechanics*, often performed by the actors in groups and applied to the performance of the entire play. Remember how classical eighteenth-century actors derived their acting poses from Greek statues? Meyerhold took his vocabulary of actors' movements from the twentieth-century aesthetic of the machine. Under his instruction, performers rotated like ball-bearings, swung their arms like hinges, and connected their bodies together like gears. The ensemble became a living machine for the performance of the play.

This embodiment of a person as part of a machine-like social group echoed avant-garde hopes in newly Communist Russia that a new and freer person—like a new and freer art—could be manufactured scientifically. However, unlike Socialist Realism, Meyerhold's approach included satire and maintained individual points of view. A basic principle of biomechanics was that the actor remain aware of his own outline within the whole stage picture. Meyerhold was eager to have the performer turn his organizing intelligence to this awareness, rather than becoming united with the role his body was performing.

Lenin rewarded Meyerhold for his early loyalty by appointing him commissar in charge of dramatic repertory and acting styles. In his new position of power, Meyerhold was Oedipally ungracious enough to snipe a little at Stanislavsky for his old-fashioned ways. But Meyerhold's challenging work baffled the peasants whose support was necessary to continue the Soviet regime. Lenin's wife wrote little notes to Meyerhold suggesting "improvements" to ensure that the factory workers and farmers who were attending performances would understand what they were seeing.

When Stalin came to power, Meyerhold was deeply in trouble. Stalin wanted an art that could be understood by peasants and he didn't want any fancy stuff, either; just good old realism allied with socialism—Socialist Realism, you could call it. (And they did, if you remember from Chapter 3.) Meyerhold protested, with predictable results. The censors wouldn't allow his productions to premiere. Stanislavsky, whose realistic aesthetic was swallowed whole by Socialist Realism, used his prestige to protect his former student as best he could, which wasn't much. In June 1939, after Meyerhold defended himself at a meeting of the directors' union, he was taken away and disappeared so completely inside a Moscow prison it wasn't even known exactly how and when he died.

It is no accident that Brecht, and not Meyerhold, became the spokesman for episodic technique. The Russian government systematically erased the record of Meyerhold's work from history. Meyerhold's writings stayed unpublished; Stanislavsky's were promoted and publicized. By the end of the Second World War, Meyerhold had become, like many Russian cultural pioneers, a whispered ghost.

Piscator began "epic" theater in an attempt to construct a German version of Meyerhold's techniques and political commitment to socialism. Brecht had seen Meyerhold's work when it was on tour in Berlin in 1930, and then later on in Moscow. But neither Brecht nor Piscator were interested in the vocabulary of a physical style, and biomechanics withered on the vine.

Meyerhold's reputation has been slowly but surely rehabilitated in Russia. Beginning in the 1960s, his writing was published, first in English, then in Russian. Although most of Meyerhold's continuing influence is as a director rather than an acting teacher, biomechanics is once again taught in Russia as well as abroad. Its practices have motivated such adherents of "physical acting" as the influential head of the International School of Theatre Anthropology, Eugenio Barba, as well as others who would fuse the energies of dance, mime, and text-driven theater. In the 1980s the Meyerhold family home was turned into a museum. Visiting the museum today, one can view the everyday articles from the house—including childhood photographs and the piano—that neighbors had hoarded (stolen?) as if they were relics of a saint.* They were subsequently returned once there was a place to display them with respect. The museum includes a large video library, photographs of Meyerhold's productions, models of the scenery, costumes (some original), and a copy of Meyerhold's death certificate next to a painting depicting him standing naked in front of a brick wall, about to be shot.

Piscator in America

Erwin Piscator wisely decided against ever actually going to the German-speaking theater he was planning for Central Asia, and so avoided arrest and murder by Stalin's

---

*The day of Meyerhold's arrest, and just before the secret police arrived, the film director Sergei Eisenstein, who had been Meyerhold's student, spirited Meyerhold's Moscow possessions to his own dacha.

agents. Many of his dedicated comrades—patiently trudging around the Central Asian plains in a wagon in the hope that Piscator would arrive—were not so lucky. When Piscator left Moscow in 1936, he went first to Paris, then took up an offer to stage an adaptation of *War and Peace* on Broadway. The production fell through and Piscator accepted another invitation, to teach at the New School for Social Research in New York City. There he organized a curriculum for professional students and child actors that emphasized the use of opposition in handling texts, and a direct, simple approach to playing the events of a scene.

Piscator was generous with his power. He was the first to hire Lee Strasberg and Stella Adler as acting teachers, although he must have been uncomfortable with some of their methods. Piscator's students went on to become influential professionals: the names claimed as alumni include Walter Matthau, Tony Curtis, Harry Belafonte, Marlon Brando, Rod Steiger, Sylvia Miles, Bea Arthur, Elaine Stritch, and Judith Malina of the Living Theatre.*

As a director, Piscator's productions—Shaw's *Saint Joan* in Washington, among them—were considered too high-minded for American audiences (Harold Clurman's opinion), and met with little success. What little other commercial work came Piscator's way he walked out on, refusing, for example, to attend the opening of his Broadway debut. He had plans for a Jewish theater in Prague and a national Mexican theater, but these projects never materialized. Like a number of German artists who came to America as refugees, including Georg Grosz, Piscator lost his impetus without the springboard of an outrage to protest. He did enjoy the creature comforts of America, among them an expensive broadcloth top coat that he wore open so that its mink lining would be conspicuous. A student called him a "talking Communist, a living Capitalist, and a practicing Fascist" (42).

Piscator's relations with Brecht during this time were problematic. Among other things, Piscator found out that Brecht had smilingly gone behind his back to secure copyrights to a property Piscator assumed was his: their successful 1928 Berlin adaptation of the Czech novel *The Good Soldier Schweyk*.† Nevertheless, in 1945 Piscator began to stage Brecht's episodic *Fear and Misery of the Third Reich* under a new title, *The Private Life of the Master Race*. When Brecht visited rehearsals, he was less than enthusiastic and Piscator quit. The exchange of letters reveals their habitual temperaments (43). Piscator's, for some reason, are written in English!

> Dear Mr. Brecht,‡
> You came late, not to say too late, and your presence didn't help to achieve results and to simplify the complications. . . . when I direct I need the time for myself without your co-directing—and when you direct you need the time without me . . . I suggest that you take over the directing, and I withdraw . . .

---

*Matthau was asked to leave, Belafonte was so miserable at the school that he left after a semester, and Brando got a job just before he was thrown out for lack of discipline.

†Piscator wanted to make a *Schweyk* movie. Brecht, who was aware of these plans, wanted Kurt Weill to collaborate on a Broadway musical version. The legal difficulties scared away investors.

‡They had known each other for over twenty years by this time.

Brecht's sunny answer:

> Dear Pis,
> The ghastly thing is that time is too short to allow one to think out theoretical disagreements.

Brecht thanks Piscator for "preventing anybody from getting the . . . impression that we have become bitter enemies." Piscator's reply, after seeing the show:

> Dear Bert:
> At different moments the other evening I wanted to jump over the footlights, come backstage, and beat you. Not because I personally felt insulted when I saw the results of this work, but at the more objective harm you have done yourself . . .

After this, they never worked together, although they acknowledged their debts to each other publicly as well as privately.

The Living Newspaper

At the time that Piscator was working in America, the United States hatched its own home-grown version of episodic acting. The Living Newspaper, a production of the Federal Theater Project, toured the United States from 1935 to 1939 and played to millions of Americans (44). The performances of the Living Newspaper theatricalized social issues—from slums (*One-Third of a Nation*) to syphilis (*Spirochete*)—with fully researched scripts and elaborate sets. More significantly, and without much theorizing, American actors were encouraged to work in a style of *reportage*; even "realistic scenes" were understood to be in the context of episodes, the way a newspaper article would quote dialogue.

America's Living Newspaper disbanded when the Federal Theater Project had its funds taken away by a Congress worried that the Project's performances of political theater led audiences to criticize the system that had allowed slums and syphilis to proliferate. Sympathy for a problem was fine, but asking questions about how to stop such problems was another thing.* The attacks on the Federal Theater Project by a so-called "House Committee to Investigate Un-American Activities" concluded—without proof, without research, and without corroboration—that "a rather large number" of Federal Theater Project employees were either members of or sympathetic to the Communist party (44). It was suspicious that the head of the Project had been in Europe attending theatrical productions—including those by Meyerhold and Piscator—and in Communist

---

*In 1928, the same thing happened to a similar group in Russia, the Blue Blouses, when Stalin decided that the only possible Communist form of acting would be Socialist Realism's embrace of Stanislavsky. What Stalin really objected to was Blue Blouses's satirical take on contemporary government policy. So it was with the Living Newspaper in America. "Satire is what closes on Saturday night" is the showbiz adage. Now you know why.

Russia, at that. One senator listed titles that "definitely bear the trademark of red Russia in their titles, plays spewed forth from the gutters of the Kremlin" (44). Among these dangerous and indecent titles was Molière's *The School for Wives*.* These farcical hearings were an unnoticed dress rehearsal for what was to follow ten years later in the form of what has been called a witch hunt for phantom Communists, not just in the American theater (although there was more than enough of that), but throughout the country.

In 1951, at the height of the Congressional hunt for Communists, Piscator (who was literally a card-carrying member of the party) returned to Europe to stage plays in Germany, Switzerland, Italy, Sweden, and the Netherlands. He was considered for a number of positions at German provincial theaters, but was repeatedly rejected. Piscator was refused so many jobs in Germany that he drew up a note to himself asking whether he had lost his talent or whether his audiences had changed. In 1957 it was his fortunes that changed, and Piscator spent the next five years running West Berlin's Freie Volksbühne. There he staged celebrated world premieres of then-contemporary German plays, among them Rolf Hochhuth's *The Deputy*—refused by other theaters because of its provocative politics portraying the Vatican's relative silence during the Second World War. Piscator died in 1966 in a nursing home after a gall bladder operation, rumor had it after a heated argument with a playwright.

Like Meyerhold, Piscator's influences as a director and stage designer are more obvious and easier to write about than his influence on the actor's thinking, but his innovations in acting technique have entered history in the performances of documentary theater throughout the world. The Living Newspaper has been resurrected in America by varying political theaters. Among many other examples, there are the Living Theatre's continuing performances on the subject of capital punishment called *Not in My Name*, presented every time there is a public execution in America.

Brecht in Exile

Out of Berlin and to France, then to Sweden then to Russia then to Finland, by 1941 Brecht ended up in—of all places—Santa Monica, California. *We changed countries more often than shoes* goes one of his poems (45). Brecht had little interest in learning to speak English,† and less interest in learning about Hollywood politics. Despite good efforts from well-connected friends, he didn't get much work in California, and he didn't want to stay there.

A good story of Brecht in Santa Monica: one day a group of friends took him to see the wonders of the Pacific Coast. They drove north, past magnificent beaches and majestic trees. Brecht smoked a smelly cigar and continued to talk without looking out

---

*The committee was chaired by a Republican Texan congressman in whose district there was a "poll tax," i.e., one paid to be able to vote. It was estimated at the time that he had been elected by less than 9 percent of the electorate. The North Carolina Democrat who made the "spewed forth from the gutters of the Kremlin" remark had a similar relationship to democracy.

†Although he could read it: many books in Brecht's personal library were in English.

of the window. When they got back into town and they were nearing the Santa Monica pier, Brecht made everyone be quiet so he could pay close attention to what was going on between a crowd of sailors and prostitutes.

Aside from the forced leisure time, which bored him, the most significant thing that happened to Brecht in America was his collaboration with the English actor Charles Laughton. The two respected each other, and Brecht set about adapting his play *Galileo* specifically for Laughton to perform the leading role. Neither man spoke the language of the other, which provided a fine opportunity for Laughton and Brecht to mime the episodes and establish the *gests* of the play. It took them three and a half years. Laughton as Galileo opened in 1947 at the Coronet Theater in Los Angeles and on Broadway in New York the following year. The production was received with respect, but nothing more. Like Piscator's productions, *Galileo*'s politics were unappealing to American audiences enjoying newfound prosperity after a ten-year depression and the Second World War.

Before *Galileo* opened in New York, the House Un-American Activities Committee, ten years after it had closed down the Federal Theater Project (and no more educated than before), invited Mr. Brecht to Washington to discuss his politics with them. Brecht had rehearsed with friends before he arrived (his performance included stalling for time while puffing on a cigar), and his responses befuddled the committee (45).

FACELESS BUREAUCRAT ACTING ON BEHALF OF TROGLODYTE SENATORS ACCU-
   RATELY REPRESENTING THE POORLY EDUCATED CONSTITUENTS WHO
   ELECTED THEM Mr. Brecht, have you ever applied to be a member of the
   Communist party?
BERTOLT BRECHT No, no, no, no, no, no, never.

When asked about his marching songs, included in an American Communist songbook:

   FB Did you write that, Mr. Brecht?
   BB No, I wrote a German poem. But that is very different from this. (*laughter*)

The first statement is, of course, literally true. Not that Brecht joined the Communist party, but he could have become a member of the party without applying. The second statement could mean any number of things, and throughout his testimony Brecht repeated that he wrote in German and couldn't really claim to be responsible for what the committee was reading in English. Brecht's testimony is such a good example of playing an opposition that the British-born critic and heroic Brecht translator Eric Bentley adapted the transcript into a play. Parts of Brecht's testimony are performed even now at the Berliner Ensemble as part of an anthology of his writing called, in German, *Die Brecht Akte*, compiled by the American actor George Tabori.

The day after his committee appearance Brecht went back to Europe. But not to Germany, no fool he. To Switzerland, where, in 1948, he waited to see what would happen in his native country. In Switzerland he staged *Mother Courage*. While the Berlin Wall was going up, Brecht staged, again in Switzerland, an adaptation of *Antigone*, Sophocles's tragedy on the subject of personal ethics and civic responsibility. The West

German government offered him a theater. The East German government offered him a theater too,* and a paid company of actors. What do you think he did? Of course, he moved to East Germany, but he kept his money in a Swiss bank and he retained an Austrian passport.

The Berliner Ensemble

For the next eight years Brecht ran the Berliner Ensemble and staged the plays he had been brooding over in sunny Santa Monica. He entered yet another period, that of reinterpreting and adapting classic texts into epic and episodic versions: *Coriolanus*, *The Recruiting Officer*, some Molière, and others. His wife Helene Weigel, who had stayed with Brecht throughout his many infidelities, was often the leading actress in these productions.

Throughout this time the East German Communist party criticized his work for not resembling Stanislavsky's. Brecht's decision to locate to East Germany was a propaganda triumph, but his theatrical ideas proved an embarrassment to the Communist regime promoting Socialist Realism. Trying to assuage their patrons, Weigel and Brecht went so far as to claim that their work had some resemblance to Stanislavsky's, but the party hacks weren't buying it. When the Berliner Ensemble toured to Moscow, Communist party critics castigated Brecht's company for its resemblance to Meyerhold's. Of course, they didn't mention Meyerhold's name; they alluded to the "failed formalism of the twenties" (45).

The political solution was to send the theater on tour outside of the Communist orbit, like goods manufactured for foreign consumption but dangerous to keep at home. Beginning in 1943, and for almost sixty years since (and still going strong), the British-born critic Eric Bentley has championed Brecht in America, translating the plays into English and writing influential essays. He also arranged for the production of Brecht's *Private Life of the Master Race* that Piscator walked out on. Bentley was a personal friend of Brecht's, and as a young man he stayed as a house guest with Brecht in Santa Monica while *Galileo* was in rehearsal. Bentley quietly differed from Brecht in several fundamental ways. In a postscript to his *Brecht Memoir* (1989), Bentley makes the fascinating comment that his unspoken differences—he was gay, at first pacifist, then anti-Communist—actually helped Bentley to understand Brecht better than those who shared Brecht's personal values. When the Berliner Ensemble's tour of *Mother Courage* played London and Paris, Bentley was joined in his efforts by Roland Barthes in France and Kenneth Tynan in England.

Among intellectuals, the Berliner Ensemble was added to the Moscow Art Theater as a place of pilgrimage. Although Brecht's works as a writer, director, and acting theoretician were collected, printed, photographed, and translated throughout the world, his plays were not often performed in Communist countries—including East Germany—until he was safely dead.

---

*Actually, they offered him someone else's theater—which Brecht accepted while he waited for his own, the present Berliner Ensemble, to be renovated.

After Brecht died, the Berliner Ensemble continued under Helene Weigel's leadership. Apocryphal rumor has it she fired almost all the actresses, not out of jealousy, but because their primary responsibility—sleeping with Brecht—was no longer necessary. After Weigel died in 1971, the revolutionary forms of the Berliner Ensemble froze. After the reunification of Germany in 1992, the political mission of the company grew questionable and funding from the state declined. In the summer of 1999, the company decided to disband and reform with a new identity. Ironically, the Ensemble's last performances were in California.

In the year 2000, the Berliner Ensemble shifted its emphasis to premieres of texts by living German authors, although the company performs the biographical *Die Brecht Akte*, and maintains as a signature piece in its repertory Brecht's version of *Richard III* that is set—like *In the Jungle of Cities*—in Chicago, and called, after its central character, *Arturo Ui*. *Arturo Ui* at the Berliner Ensemble is performed in the Heiner Müller staging of 1964, which emphasizes the character's resemblance to Adolf Hitler. In April 2000, a performance of *Arturo Ui* held on Hitler's one hundred and eleventh birthday began outside the theater with an actor delivering a repetitive speech (written by Hitler himself) over a microphone in a Nazi-era squawk from a balcony to the street. Inside the theater, the actor in the Richard role, a popular television performer, began on all fours like a dog, barking and growling. The progression of episodes was quite clear: a wild beast rises to become a lord among men. The equivalent of Richard's scene with Lady Anne took place with the Richard character raping the widow on top of the corpse of her dead husband (not father-in-law), the widow's head between the corpse's splayed doll legs—a very clear *gest*, simultaneously funny and grotesque.

Brecht's Influence

In England

Brecht's point of view and politics were formed after the collapse of the Kaiser's Germany in the First World War. They resonated in England after the collapse of the British Empire and the reorganization of British life following the Second World War. Thus, so far, Brecht's major influence among professional actors and directors has been in England. His techniques offer new insight into the interpretation, staging, and acting of the classic texts that are the core of the British repertory system. Mindful of Brecht, British directors like Joan Littlewood and Peter Brook taught their actors the basic skills of episodic performance. Littlewood's productions, in particular, stressed ensemble work, clear *gests*, and direct address, not only in productions of Brecht's plays, but in the performances of new plays by modern British writers.

British playwrights capitalized on the abilities of British actors to perform a role within an episode just as American playwrights capitalized on the technical skills of American actors trained to perform emotional recall. Among the post-war British playwrights who wrote episodic texts with oppositional characters: Harold Pinter, Edward Bond, and Tom Stoppard. The style has been especially useful for those playwrights, like

Caryl Churchill and David Hare, who question traditional British society's assignment of roles to women, poor people, and minorities.

In the continuing struggle around the world

Episodic theater renews itself as part of social struggle in third-world countries. In Brazil and the Philippines, in Africa and India, political theaters have adapted Brecht's techniques to perform texts in indigenous as well as colonial languages. News accounts of slaughter, presentation of national heroes, and reenactments of grand historical times are performed in villages throughout the world on open ground between mud huts—with the intention of inciting political action. Approaches to theater in the Philippines (46) and in a number of African countries, among them Tanzania, Kenya, Zimbabwe, and the Union of South Africa have included episodic techniques modeled on approaches from Eastern Europe and Communist China (47).

Episodic Acting With and Without Brecht

In America

Recognized or not, episodic structure organizes such disparate American playwrights as Sam Shepard, Gertrude Stein, and Thornton Wilder. Established political theaters in America, such as the rural Bread and Puppet, the San Francisco Mime Company, and the Living Theatre (thriving since 1947; its co-artistic director Judith Malina studied with Piscator), all combine social activism with episodic acting techniques. The technique of playing episodes is taught at influential and official conservatories.

Because Brecht was a Communist, his influence was kept quiet among his Hollywood connections. When the RDF—the French equivalent of England's BBC radio—asked Charles Laughton for a quote about Brecht on the occasion of Brecht's death, Laughton dodged the interview and avoided the possibility of getting himself entangled in the House Un-American Activities Committee.

Acknowledged or not, Charles Laughton's ideas of performance had altered after his three and a half years with Brecht. The one film Laughton directed, *The Night of the Hunter* (1955), can be viewed as a checklist of episodic skills. *Opposition* organizes the acting throughout. Robert Mitchum plays a preacher who murders widows so he may use their money to praise God. *L-O-V-E* is tattooed on the knuckles of the preacher's right hand, and *H-A-T-E* on the knuckles of his left. In one sequence, the two hands wrestle with each other, *alienating* the struggle inside the hypocrite. In public, the preacher is kind and gentle with women, in private he humiliates his new wife. The couple's relationship is established by a *gest* on their honeymoon night. After the preacher humiliates his bride, he rolls over in bed facing away from her. Shelley Winters, who studied acting with Laughton, plays the bride (in the year before her performance in *A Place in the Sun*).

The characters often perform their roles reluctantly, like the hangman who washes

56

his hands after a day's work and wishes aloud he had some other line of business. The wide-eyed Lillian Gish from the silent film *Orphans of the Storm* plays a rescuer of orphans—who packs a rifle. Almost all the shots are stagy and include crowds, families, or groups that give the individual figure significance within a social setting. The hangman's wife is seen behind the sink, disapproving of her husband's scruples. The screenplay, credited to James Agee, is an adaptation of the 1953 novel by Davis Grubb, and often incorporates tableaux. One vivid shot shows Winters sitting dead under the water with her throat slit and her hair trailing—remarkably similar to an image out of a ballad Brecht sang in a Berlin cabaret many years before. The actors (Mitchum excepted) seem to be following Laughton's direction without completely understanding what it is they're being asked to do.

To watch actors using episodic techniques with an awareness that they are doing so, study any one of the performances in Martin Scorsese's *Raging Bull* (1980), the biographical story of the heavyweight boxer Jake La Motta. Although it was shot in black and white, the film contains a few scenes presented as faded color "home movies" with the actors playing directly—but silently—to the camera: waving and mugging, obviously aware that they are creating something artificial. One character gets married, another has children, and these episodes in the story are communicated by *gests*: a ring on the hand, a baby on the lap.

The riveting performance given by Robert De Niro in the role of Jake La Motta is a dynamic opposition of self-doubt and aggression. His identity is a series of often contradictory roles: winner, loser, lover, scold, bewildered animal, cocky braggart. In the last scene, the former champion, now down on his luck, prepares for a nightclub appearance. Sitting in his seedy dressing room and looking into the mirror (his face is reflected inside a square reminiscent of a boxing ring), La Motta delivers a long monologue from Budd Schulberg's script for the film *On the Waterfront* (1954), alienating the words of the text—with what amounts to a caption—by first announcing: "Some People Aren't That Lucky."

Smoking on a cigar, De Niro recites the words to the speech in a stilted and awkward way, including *I could have been a contender*—a line made famous in *On the Waterfront* when delivered by Marlon Brando as a passionate cry. The meaning of the text and the parallel to the character's situation are inferred by the movie audience and De Niro, but not by the emotional situation of the La Motta character. The image of a boxer in a ring as a metaphor for life can, of course, be found throughout Brecht's writings on the theater (as well as in *In the Jungle of Cities*), but no direct or indirect link—not even the cigar—is necessary to explain the use of oppositions, *gests*, and alienation. After all, the use of episodic techniques in film dates back to the beginning of the medium.

In the cinema

When the invention of cinema created a new venue for acting, performers called on episodic technique to satisfy the technical demands of recording scenes on film. To begin with, the inability of the early equipment to record sound meant film scripts replaced dialogue with scenarios that described events to be performed in front of the camera, often through improvisations. The lack of sound forced actors to establish episodes clearly, without words.

An early film canister could hold only enough film to record a sequence lasting one minute. Even as late as 1949, the maximum duration of a shot was less than ten minutes. Short sections, then and now, were compiled into a sequence, but only later, after the performers had concluded their work. Directors could, did, and do ask actors to play the middle of a performance before the beginning. Working out of sequence, it was impossible for an actor to play a *through-line*; it was necessary to perform the event to be recorded by the camera as a separate unit, or episode.

As in any theatrical episodic performances, the episode of a film needs to be understood in common by an ensemble. The director, the performer, and the technicians must all agree what the point of the shot is before the film is exposed to record it. Lillian Gish worked in film until she was ninety. Remember the seven-year-old Lillian's first and only acting lesson? *Speak loudly and clearly so that everyone in the theater can hear you—or they'll get another little girl who can.* That sums up the intention of episodic acting: play so that everyone in the theater understands. Seven years old or seventy, on stage or in front of the camera, that's your job as a performer.

In the future

The demands of videotape, performance art, and rapid editing techniques continue to transform what an actor is expected to contribute to a performance. Playing episodes, cooperation within the ensemble to perform each episode, and the subordination of character to a role within an episode are the essentials of episodic acting. These reappear no matter what new venues for performance appear.

Yet there is no single written source, like Stanislavsky's, for actors to learn the vocabulary of episodic acting. Brecht's writing on the epic theater is theoretical and aimed at directors and writers much more than actors. His practical advice is sketchy and often contradictory. Along with Brecht's charts and essays in *Brecht on Theater*, the excellent critical biographies of Brecht, among them Martin Esslin's *Brecht, The Man and His Work* (1971) and *Brecht for Beginners* (1984) written by Michael Thoss, need to be combed through for something as simple as the practical application of alienation.

Any examination of Brecht and his system often drifts into a distracting discussion of the plays and the fascinating contradictions of Brecht's life. This book has fallen into the trap as well, but Brecht's life experience colors his ideas to such an extent that you need to understand that experience before you can extract or discount, say, the Marxist basis for transactions.

Alhough Brecht is not the only master of episodic theater, others don't offer much in print. Piscator wrote very little about his objective theater. His students and colleagues wrote less. What few books there are report on the physical productions and extol the political mission, rather than extol the reportage of the actors.* Meyerhold,

---

*The exception to this, and the fullest account, appears in John Willet's out-of-print *The Theatre of Erwin Piscator* (Holmes & Meier Publishers, 1979).

though he went so far as to set up schools to train student actors, never lived long enough to complete a technique book for performers. His ideas for such a thing can be gleaned from his collected essays *Meyerhold on Theater* (1969) and Alexander Gladkov's *Meyerhold Speaks, Meyerhold Rehearses* (1997). What has been published since is about Meyerhold's staging techniques—rather than his acting—and mostly concerns itself, understandably, with reviving biomechanics.

These chapters aim to rescue episodic acting from its history, its politics, and the lives of its founders. Episodic acting will always be around, and needs to be studied, practiced, and developed further.

One more story from Brecht's Santa Monica exile: While she was watching rehearsals for Laughton's *Galileo*, Shelley Winters noticed a German janitor picking up pieces of paper in the back of the theater and putting them in the trash. She felt sorry for him and brought him to meet her parents, who spoke German. The janitor returned weekly for Shelley's father's Friday night card game. Years later, when she went to see George Tabori's *Die Brecht Akte* in New York (where it was called *Brecht on Brecht*), Winters realized from a photograph that was hanging on the proscenium arch that the janitor was the playwright. She called her mother. "Mr. Brechstein? We always thought he was a costume jeweler." When asked what he did in the old country, Brecht had told Shelley's parents: "I made jewels for poor people" (48).*

Brecht was using an *image* to describe himself—our next subject at hand.

---

*Winters writes: "He always looked lonely and hungry" (48).